The Gospel of Grace

for Wounded Sojourners

The Gospel of Grace for Wounded Sojourners

Sermonic Reflections on Hope in Christ

Albert J. D. Walsh

WIPF & STOCK · Eugene, Oregon

THE GOSPEL OF GRACE FOR WOUNDED SOJOURNERS
Sermonic Reflections on Hope in Christ

Copyright © 2014 Albert J. D. Walsh. All rights reserved. Except for brief quotations in critical publications or reviews, no part of this book may be reproduced in any manner without prior written permission from the publisher. Write: Permissions. Wipf and Stock Publishers, 199 W. 8th Ave., Suite 3, Eugene, OR 97401.

Unless otherwise noted, all Scripture quotations are taken from the Holman Christian Standard Bible®, Copyright © 1999, 2000, 2002, 2003, 2009 by Holman Bible Publishers. Used by permission. Holman Christian Standard Bible®, Holman CSB®, and HCSB® are federally registered trademarks of Holman Bible Publishers.

Wipf and Stock
An Imprint of Wipf and Stock Publishers
199 W. 8th Ave., Suite 3
Eugene, OR 97401

www.wipfandstock.com

ISBN 13: 978-1-62564-626-2

Manufactured in the U.S.A. 05/30/2014

Contents

Preface | *vii*
Foreword by Drake Williams III | *xi*
Introduction | *xiii*

One
Luke 15:1–6: The Shepherd King | 1

Two
1 Corinthians 1:4–9: Nothing is Lacking | 8

Three
Philippians 2:5–11: The Admirable Exchange | 13

Four
Luke 2:1–14: Holiness in Human Flesh | 18

Five
Mark 15:16–32: Haunted by the Cross of Christ | 22

Six
John 20:24–25: "Setting the Record Straight" | 26

Seven
John 20:27–28: Rejoicing in the Wounds of Christ | 31

Eight
John 2:1–3: Celebrating a Kingdom | 36

Nine
John 15:4: Fruit of the Vine | 41

Ten
Matthew 19:13: The Touch of Christ | 46

Eleven
John 21:4–5: Morning Came | 51

Twelve
John 13:34–35: Our Heritage | 56

Thirteen
Mark 1:38–39: He Came Preaching | 60

Fourteen
John 18:36: Christ's Kingdom | 66

Fifteen
Luke 21:25–28: Faint from Fear | 72

Sixteen
Luke 2:51–52: He Obeyed His Parents | 77

Seventeen
Luke 4:16–19: The Claim of Christ | 82

Eighteen
Luke 4:28–30: How do we hear Him | 86

Nineteen
Luke 9:30–31: Another Exodus | 92

Twenty
Luke 4:1–13: The Devil You Say! | 97

Twenty-One
John 2:1–12: Why Wine? | 103

Conclusion | 109

Preface

THE FOLLOWING SERMONIC REFLECTIONS were preached over a period of several years and before the gracious listeners who worshipped in a variety of different settings. I have found most church-community members to be the heart and soul of Christian sincerity, seeking to make their way along the path of discipleship with all of the struggles, set-backs, sorrows, and incredible joys associated with this sojourning, which is so common to Christian believers. They have listened attentively and with all good grace to sermon upon sermon, and have been generous in their support of their pastor's every effort to explicate the Holy Scriptures, hoping as he does to bridge the span between words that are centuries in existence and the wounds and worries as fresh as the morning news—enabling the Holy Spirit to speak through the preacher's own feeble and often faltering words. At our best, we who assume the pulpit each and every Lord's Day make the genuine attempt to bring the "whole counsel of God" to bear on the commonalities of Christian discipleship, which we have witnessed being worked-out in and through the lives of the saints of God placed in our charge.

Pastors who have been preaching for years know only too well how their words, on any given Sunday, are the result of that labor of love which begins with the chosen text and ends with the final "Amen." Between the choice of text and the final draft of any sermon there is the life of the congregation, evident in the daily and numerous encounters with those individual members who have opened their lives to their pastor. In the process of preparation

Preface

he or she sees the faces, hears the voices, and remembers how this "word" he or she preaches is intended to speak directly to the deepest needs of these "wounded-sojourners." And we are all, each of us, wounded! Life is one long road of reckless choices, reasons for rejoicing, deep regrets, and learning that we really do "reap" as we have "sown." The sermon is not so much a lecture on the art of theological insight, as it is a report from the frontlines of faith where one encounters those who are wounded-sojourners—like a mirror image of one's own sainted-self—and is a proclamation issued in the midst of the battle that victory has been won and will one day be tasted by those who have remained in the trenches of the righteous—sojourning saints who bear their wounds with such grace and good will as only God can create and sustain in the human soul. The person in the pew is the stalwart-saint who comes each Lord's Day seeking—what? Simply (or perhaps it is not simple at all!) to have the "balm of Gilead" applied to the festering wounds of faith, so that he or she can return to the "fray" with a rejuvenated sense of the purpose for which he or she has been called—enlisted, if you will—by the One who carries the banner of victory to the front.

As long as the Church of Jesus Christ battles-on—not, we are reminded, against "flesh and blood," but against those unseen "spiritual forces"—there will be a need for preaching, for the ministry of proclamation, for feeding the "troops" of God's own army with the real "manna from heaven" in the form of the human word-as-witness that becomes the Word of God under the inspiration and empowerment of God's Holy Spirit. We make no pretense to these sermonic reflections being of value to those who remain outside the life of Christ's ecclesia, but would hope that—at the very least—such readers would remain open to the possibility that something in this offer would (by God's grace alone!) speak to their human heart and soul, and perhaps even heal the wounds they have borne for so long and alone!

These sermonic reflections are offered to the wider ecclesia in honor of those brothers and sisters at Heidelberg who have sat so patiently and listened so attentively to their pastor's preaching.

Perhaps these—my friends in Christ—will one day bear testimony to having tasted something of that "heavenly manna" in and through their pastor's efforts to proclaim the Word of God 'in season and out of season," and always to the greater glory of the Triune God.

Foreword

THE *GOSPEL OF GRACE for Wounded Sojourners* is a collection of sermons on well-known themes from the Scriptures. Sermons are naturally delivered to a congregation on a particular day and in a particular setting. Certain sermons, however, step beyond the time barrier and are worthy of being published so that readers from many different backgrounds can be inspired by them in any setting. These messages are of that caliber.

Most of those who attend church will be familiar with the texts discussed in each of these messages. They certainly, will be familiar with the major Christian holidays that are referenced. Few, however, have the benefit of hearing the perspective of a seasoned pastor with many life experiences who continues to author thoughtful books on pastoral issues. In his 32 years of ordained ministry, Albert Walsh has displayed deep thinking about the Christian faith. He has written about important Christian topics such as: the Eucharist, death and dying, grace, faith, and freedom. He has thought about these particular texts for many years.

A particular facet that makes these messages appealing is the interest that Albert Walsh has in ecumenical theology. He has persistently pursued dialogue around the common creeds of the Christian faith throughout his career. His landmark work in this field is *United and Uniting: An Ecumenical Ecclesiology for a Church in Crisis*. While others are interested in an ecumenicity that stretches beyond creeds, Albert Walsh has consistently promoted ecumenicity within these boundaries.

Foreword

This perspective makes a difference when he arrives at familiar texts and topics. He highlights truths that Christians from many different backgrounds will accept. Yet, these truths fall decidedly within the framework of the early Christian confessions.

One other aspect distinguishes these writings. They are the reflections of one who is a fellow sojourner. While many within the ministry present themselves on a higher level than their followers, Albert Walsh is conscious of being a fellow traveler on the way to glory. His writing is of one who comes alongside to help rather than of the professional or expert dispensing opinions.

I commend these sermons to your reading. By reading these, may you be helped in your spiritual journey!

Drake Williams III

Introduction

THERE ARE NUMEROUS MANUALS and extensive theological explications available on the art of homiletics (i.e. preaching as proclamation), and the reader would do well to refer to any one of them should he or she be looking for a more formal approach to the preaching ministry, or a more concise analysis of what is required of the one who must occupy the pulpit on a regular basis. That is not our purpose in this *Introduction*. Instead, we want to offer some general reflections on preaching from the perspective of one who has been engaged in this ministry for more than thirty years of service in pastoral office.

Of the obligations and responsibilities that fall within the purview of the pastoral office, none is more vital than the event of proclamation in the context of the worshiping congregation; there can be no skimping on the fundamental preparations required of this particular event. Such preparations will include the obvious attention to commentary, word study, etc.; but there is the centrality of equal time, attention, and dedication given to maturation in theological depth. Over time the pastor will deepen in his or her knowledge of both the traditional theological and doctrinal explications, and at their best with ecumenical expansiveness, and the related biblical, liturgical, and ethical concerns of his or her own time; seeking to become ever more mature in the capacity to articulate a theological position with clarity.

For the pastor there can be no division between preacher and teacher, and therefore there can be no division of labor between

Introduction

preparation for preaching and the wider interests of Christian education—(we would prefer *discipleship formation*)—as both forms of ministry demand a depth of knowledge of both biblical and theological exposition over the long and richly variegated history of the Christian faith—both East and West. While there are some who would argue that the model for contemporary pastoral ministry that will best serve the needs of the congregation is the Board Room, the reality is that the Church catholic is desperately in need of pastors who spend as much (if not more) time in their study as they do attending to the administrative needs of local ministry.

The deepest needs of the person in the pew are not the felt needs, which are often inadequately expressed to begin with, but the more desperate demand for attentiveness to the woundedness of the human heart and soul. There is a weariness evident on the face and in the body language of the person sitting in the pew, a weariness that comes from the long walk taken between Sunday and Sunday in a world that has grown increasingly cold and indifferent to things divine, sacred, deeper than the surface of one's skin— even the skin of the human heart. It is clearly no secret that our contemporary cultural and social setting—indeed, worldwide—is awash in an ambiance of cynicism and doubt, and a shrinking global setting that has not contributed to a deepening awareness of interdependence and the need for a communal-consciousness.

The most common characteristics of communal existence (e.g. acceptance, mutuality of respect, shared hopes, compassionate-care for the other) seem to have fallen into the abyss of self-assertion and promotion of a hybrid form of individualism, offered as the safeguard against the loss of one's *self*—which is itself an assertion of *personal rights* over the interests and concerns of the larger *communal* welfare. The person seated in the pew on any given Sunday morning has been shaped by these same cultural and social forces—and more—to the extent that church is sought as a reprieve from this onslaught. There is a genuine desire for rejuvenation and replenishment of those characteristics of life in Christ that can and will assist the weary-wounded-sojourner through yet another week in the fray.

Introduction

And we have not even touched on those experiences of human existence, shared by all, which can be attributed with inflicting their own wounds on the heart and soul: the loss of a loved one to death, the loss of employment, home, or family, the diagnosis with a terminal illness, the child whose health has become precarious at best, the constant barrage of external expectations, obligations, and responsibilities, the emotional battles that accompany all forms of relational living, not to mention the way in which each and all of these, and more, can and often do have deleterious consequences for one's sense of spiritual well-being. To paraphrase the well-known aphorism: When believers come to worship, they do not come with the expectation of hearing the latest news regarding the Hittites!

Any pastor worth his or her salt knows only too well exactly what is being sought by the saint seated in the pew—the atmosphere prior to any sermon in any church on any given Sunday morning is palpable with expectation. *Is there no Word from the Lord?* There is no one with a greater appreciation for the sincerity of this question, issuing as it does from the heart and soul of the person in the pew, than the preacher who comes to the pulpit with the sweat and blood of solemn preparation for this proclamation staining his or her stole. That same study from which the preacher has emerged is crowded with the names, faces, and—*yes*—the woundedness of those he or she has come to love in Christ; they have peered over his or her shoulder with the intent of keeping him or her honest to their deep and deliberate concerns.

Attending to this deeper demand of the human heart and soul, with pastoral sensitivity and intelligence, requires more of the one holding pastoral office than can be provided by the occasional continuing education seminar or convocation on the latest church development technique. By vow of his or her ordination, the pastor takes upon him or herself the pledge to continue to grow and mature as a theologian of the Church catholic; there can be no higher calling, no greater purpose, and no more precarious task than is that of becoming a pastoral theologian, serving the spiritual needs of God's People through preaching/teaching.

Introduction

There may be value in many of those more practical approaches to the issues facing the pastor as he or she attends to the ministry and soul-care of those placed in his or her charge; but such writings can never serve as a substitute for the hard work of theological exploration and explication; the daily reading of Scripture—for more than either devotional or homiletic-preparations—is imperative, as familiarity with this foundation has no substitute in providing the pastor with the substance of the *whole counsel of God*.

It is ludicrous to suggest that one take to the bedside of the dying member a copy of Barth's *Dogmatics*; however, it is not preposterous to affirm that the pastor who has taken the time to struggle with Barth, Anselm, Augustine, Aquinas, Calvin, and a host of early church fathers and mothers will discover a treasure-chest of truth available to him or her as he or she attends to those final moments of life and the deepest spiritual needs of his or her "sheep." That same treasure holds invaluable merit as the pastor prepares to preach—to bring before the anxious longings of the human heart the profound answer: *There is a Word from the Lord!*

The preparations for pulpit have their mirror image in what must follow each and every Sunday of proclamation, and that is the necessity to take time on a Sunday afternoon to read the same sermon reflectively, asking what might have been said differently, more clearly, or what changes need to be made to illustrative matter so that such illustration(s) could become less opaque to the biblical text itself. It is a discipline with a pay-off in eventual preparation, as the focus on the form and content of the sermon preached will eventually become the basis upon which the preacher will choose to shape any/all future sermons.

Having feedback from those in the congregation has merit of its own, but in lieu of such feedback, the practice of reflectively reading one's own work will serve to enhance awareness of those habits of preparation that can, unfortunately, end-up as redundancy in proclamation. There is a laziness in preaching that tends to (wrongly) associate wordiness with depth. Reflective reading of sermons preached holds the potential for awareness of such

Introduction

laziness in one's sermonizing. Regardless of the habits one tends to form over years of sermonizing, attention to work that has been done is helpful in providing evidence of those habits one needs to overcome.

Over the years of preaching I have become convinced that there is no one area of pastoral work that is more important than is the Sunday sermon; it is here, with the body of believers gathered in the sanctuary, that the pastor is given (by grace) the opportunity to open the Scriptures—as did our Lord with His disciples on the road to Emmaus—and to share the glorious event of listening for the Word of God in proclamation. We pastors are engaged in this most profound practice of preaching—not a lecture, or a lesson, or even a message—but a *genuine proclamation*, which by God's grace and in the empowerment of the Holy Spirit, holds the potential to move beyond *witness*—to disclose the very personal-presence of Him who is being proclaimed.

This will be seen by some as controversial, as implying that there is a sacramental characteristic to the event of preaching; even so, there is biblical and theological warrant for the contention that the Word becomes *real presence* in and through the proclamation of the Gospel—as the singular event of grace that cannot be divorced from His presence. There is a momentous aspect to this worshipful, this liturgical event, which should not be diminished to mere preaching, as opposed to the grandeur of grace evident in the sacraments of the Church catholic. In an environment in which the content of the message has become essential to all forms of media, and yet where distortion is often permitted for the sake of titillation, the event of preaching—as assertion of unadulterated *Truth*—is all the more imperative. While it cannot be asserted that, in preaching, the medium is the message, it can be affirmed without qualification that the message bears the central-character of the Messenger for those with *ears to hear*.

The concern is not to elevate the event of preaching to the level of a sacrament, but rather to affirm the theological significance of preaching as the liturgical event in which Christ speaks to His people in and through the proclamation of the Gospel and in

Introduction

the power of the Holy Spirit. In such proclamatory speech Christ's presence is known among, for, and with His people, as they gather in the name of God the Father. In this sense, then, the event of proclamation is also an event of the triune God, and the Word received in and through the witness of Scripture and preaching is recognized as the Christ of God—the living, reigning Lord of life. Christ's word is no less medicinal than it was when spoken in His incarnate life; the wounded-sojourners find that by this Word, received as proclamatory speech, the *balm of Gilead* is applied to their wounds; and where healing is not immediate, they receive the courage of faith to await future restoration as promised by their Redeemer.

While sermons are not to be read simply to glean ideas or illustrative materials for one's own efforts, and while taking portions of sermonic materials—or sermons in their entirety—cannot be considered an acceptable practice, there is advantage to the use of sermons for the purposes of devotional practice and reflection. Sermons, at their best, are always contextual, spoken to a particular time, place, and gathered body of believers; there is no sense in which any sermon can be lifted from the page and merely pasted-into-the-context of the preacher—the fit is like the skin of an elephant on a pigmy! The contextual nature of preaching limits the use of any sermon and should serve as the basis for prohibition of direct transfer from one pulpit to another. Having said that, every sermon is not the possession of the preacher him or herself, but belongs to the Church catholic and to that extent can be made available for general reflection and perhaps even as a teaching tool.

If it can be asserted that the pastor is a preacher of the Gospel in waiting, then it can also be said that the preacher is the embodiment of proclamation of the Gospel, and every event of pastoral care provides opportunity for proclamation. The pastor bears the Gospel at the core of his or her being; in the purposeful choice of a phrase, and in the course of providing pastoral care-of-souls, the pastor offers a word to strengthen a struggling soul, a word to lift-up a life that has fallen into the abyss of despair, a word intended to renew faith in the face of some seemingly insurmountable obstacle,

Introduction

a word that—under the empowerment of the Holy Spirit—resonates with the glorious Gospel of Christ. The language we employ is not our own, but has been handed-on to those who hold pastoral office; it is the language of faith that has sustained and nurtured disciples of Christ for more than two millennia; it is the language of the pulpit and the language of pastoral care-of-souls. Pastors are so very blessed to have been called to this immense undertaking and will thank God that it is the glorious burden of being yoked to Christ, the Lord who is both the giver of this incredible language and the gift itself.

The following sermons are offered for the purposes of devotional reflection and inspiration. With the exception of the first sermon in this collection, it will be noted that the order in which these sermons come in this collection is intended to portray the subtitle of this book, and therefore are representative of the glorious hope to be found in Christ, from His advent into this world and spanning the time until His return in glory. The first sermon in the collection is offered as a synoptic of the entire book. My sermonic style is to preach from a full manuscript, though I draft the manuscript in conversational format; the conjunctives, etc. of ordinary conversation have remained part of the sermons presented in this collection; it is hoped that in this way my own voice will come through to the reader. The length of each sermon text has been altered (lengthened or shortened), yet only to enhance the narrative for the purposes of greater clarity than the time allotted for preaching permitted in original context. Even so, the modifications to the text have been kept to a minimum, with the desire to maintain the original length of the work as first presented to the congregation. Modifications have also been made to the grammar, syntax, etc., but this too only for purposes of greater clarity.

May the Spirit of the Lord God speak in and through them once again, to those with *ears to hear* and hearts yearning for the healing Christ alone affords as the Good Shepherd and Great Physician of all wounded-sojourners.

One

Luke 15:1–6
The Shepherd King

All the tax collectors and sinners were approaching to listen to (Jesus). And the Pharisees and scribes were complaining, "This man welcomes sinners and eats with them!" So He told them this parable: "What man among you who has 100 sheep and loses one of them, does not leave the 99 in the open field and go after the lost one until he finds it? When he has found it, he joyfully puts it on his shoulders, and coming home, he calls his friends and neighbors together, saying to them, 'Rejoice with me, because I have found my lost sheep!'"

THE TEACHING OF JESUS and in particular as recorded in the gospel according to Luke, smacks of the ironic, the otherwise puzzling and disarming. Luke's gospel is packed with the contrary and the turn-about. And yet, so it seems to me, the nature of Scripture as a witness to the Word of God is, as a form of communication, a word that's contrary to all words, while at the same time redeeming, elevating, and complementing all other forms of human expression. Scripture itself, even as a *God-breathed* (2 Tim. 3:16), inspired text, cannot be divorced from the commonalities of normal human communication, and all of the problems associated with the limitations of language. So believe me when I say I mean no disrespect to Jesus; but I find that, as a teaching tool, the parable of the lost sheep is about as outrageous as one can get! It's illogical to imply that a responsible shepherd is one who'd leave the majority of his flock behind in the open field in order to set out in search of one wayward lamb.

On hearing this parable of Jesus we might simply shrug our shoulders, thinking nothing of the suggestion that a shepherd would leave the majority of his charge unguarded, in order to search for a simpleton who'd wandered off–God's knows why or to where–ending up lost in the threatening wilds. But that's simply because shepherding isn't the chosen profession of any one of us here in this sanctuary this evening. However, the shepherds present in Jesus' first audience would most likely have sneered at the idea that someone would deem such actions, as those represented by the character in this parable, the behavior of a responsible shepherd. This was, after all, how they made a living! It was generally the case that shepherds were hired hands, and even though generally speaking they were rough characters, they'd never think to risk the loss of an entire flock in the ridiculous attempt to search-out and save the life of one crack-pot lamb who'd wandered off into a hostile terrain. No shepherd in his right mind would've wanted that kind of foolishness on his professional résumé! Still, the implications of the parable can be lost on us simply because we're distant from and unfamiliar with the world of shepherding.

So, let's reframe. Imagine you have a jewelers shop on South Street, Philadelphia, and you've hired someone to manage the business for you. One morning your newly hired manager opens the shop only to discover that the smallest and least expensive diamond is missing from its case. Does he phone you to ask how you might want him to handle this loss? No, he leaves the shop, and all cases holding the majority of your most expensive gems, unlocked and unguarded.

Luke 15:1–6

And he sets out to comb the streets of the city searching for the one lost lower-cost diamond. Now you're notified by the Philadelphia police that your store has been burglarized, and every precious gem in the store, stolen.

You rush to the shop only to see your hired manager coming toward you with a beaming smile, "Don't worry," he says through a confident grin, "I've found that lost little gem!" Do you commend him and join him as he celebrates the find, or do you fire him for being foolish, if not negligent, in the performance of his professional duties? Or shift the image again.

Suppose you're shopping one evening at the Mall and as you get into your car, you hear the sound of a *clink* on the ground. At last check you had four pennies in your pocket; it would appear that one of the four has fallen to the ground and isn't immediately apparent to your scanning in the darkness. So, you hop in your car and drive away. That night you can't sleep a wink, worrying, thinking obsessively about that one penny. It's three in the morning; you're out there alone in the Mall parking lot, down on your hands and knees with a pocket flashlight looking for the lost penny; and you find it!

You return home, appreciative for having found that one penny! To share your joy, you plan a wild party at the Four Seasons, to the tune of $12,000, inviting all the people you know, and not a few of your neighbors. Is that the behavior of a rational person? Do you honestly believe your family, friends, and neighbors wouldn't wonder about your sanity, think you'd lost your senses, or were suffering from some form of mental breakdown?

The shepherd in search of one lost lamb is nothing short of ridiculous in the eyes of the world, his world and our own. In fact, we don't act that way, do we? I envision those shepherds who first heard this teaching of Jesus thinking the parable a farce, and the rabbi, Jesus, odd for thinking this way. That is until somewhere inside they came to the realization that He was, as they say today, on-to-something. They were—to the person—each of them, in some inexplicable fashion lost and in need of being found. And found not just by anyone, but by someone like the shepherd in the parable. What would it mean to be in the care of someone who loved like that shepherd, someone willing to risk looking ludicrous for any and every expression of this kind of penetrating and extravagant love?

Dare they hope with heart and soul—even for a moment—that there could be a love like that in the whole of the universe? No, that would be too much to ask, wouldn't it? In particular if this were a likeness of God; God would never do such a thing—would He? Even though the behavior of the shepherd does seem ludicrous, even when we realize that Jesus is talking about what God intends to do in and through Christ; that still doesn't seem to lessen the feeling that such behavior, as represented by this shepherd, is incongruous—at best.

Yes, it's actually incongruous, but only because the love of God is contrary to all that we experience of love in the world of human expectations and interactions. It's not a love born of this world, and it's not a love sustained by this world, and it's not a love natural to this world. The love of God is different from any and every expectation we have of love as disclosed and experienced in the ways of the world. And yet, I can't help but feel that we're not so different from those who first heard Jesus tell this parable. We want to believe that when we're lost, such love will come searching to save us. We want to know that we're valued in just that way and to the same degree, don't we? If you've never been lost, then I suppose there's no way you'll ever understand how important it is to know that there's *Someone* who will never give up until you've been located, lifted up in love, and brought back to the safety and security only such love can create and sustain.

The story is told of the elderly man whose sole possession to survive Katrina was his fishing boat. He spent four days without sleep, riding above the flood waters and seeking to save those stranded on roof tops. Somehow his name became public, and the lost souls of hurricane Katrina, left stranded on their roof tops, managed to write signs that read "We're trusting that George will come to save us!" Several months later everyone learned the true identity of the man for whom the signs were intended. The media

Luke 15:1–6

swarmed when he was found and asked him why he kept on seeking to save others; he said, "Because every soul is of value to God and therefore to me!"

If you've never been lost in your life then I doubt this extraordinary teaching of Jesus will make much sense to you. But I'm certain there isn't one person in this room who hasn't been *lost* at some point in his or her life, left to languish in some arid place, or stranded above the rising tide of life's threatening flood waters, hoping against hope that someone would care and come looking for you and in love. I doubt that there's one soul in this place who would survive for long if he or she believed that his or her life was of little or no value to anyone, anywhere, for anything. I'm certain it makes a difference in the world for each of us to know that regardless of the circumstance, or how it is we come to find ourselves lost, the love of Almighty God will never give up the search to save us, to bring us back, to bring us home to His divine heart.

I like to think that sometime later that day, long after the crowds of people had dispersed, and all had returned, each to his or her own home, those who heard Jesus teach this parable suddenly remembered the words of the prophet Ezekiel (chapter 34) and, discovered the words of the prophet took on a whole new meaning in light of the teaching of Jesus. Maybe we too can hear them as if for the first time. And perhaps if you're feeling lost in something even now, you'll hear the voice of One who'll never give up until He has found you and carried you to safety, because He values you as much as He does any other single lamb of His fold.

The concept of "kingship" is no less foreign to most, if not all, of us; we're sufficiently removed from the experience to have as much difficulty making sense of the exact nature of that office as we do that of "shepherd." Perhaps we could explore the way in which kingship was commonly understood in the time of Christ, and that would provide us with insight regarding how Christ's contemporaries would've understood such association, but would not necessarily help us attain greater clarity. It should be enough to state that, while kingly rule in the time of Christ was often associated with corruption of power and misuse of the status conferred upon the "king" or "Caesar" by virtue of the office held, Christ's kingly rule is measured with the qualities of justice, mercy, compassion, and love. Like the shepherd in the parable, whose behavior is contrary to the reality of shepherds in the experience of the people in the time of Christ, the kingship—or Kyrios rule—of Christ poses a striking contrast to all other forms of rule at that time. We would associate the kingly rule of Christ with harmony, joy, fullness of life for all residents of His kingdom, and a foundational love for His "subjects" that is evident, not so much in His demands placed before them, as in His own servitude—leading by example. What we have in our Lord is a "Shepherd King," wherein there is no contradiction between one form of service and the other, where an incomparable love is the basis upon which this King desires to enrich the lives of His people, as well as the establishment of a mission to nurture all of His "sheep" in the "green pastures" of His compassion and grace. As "King" Christ lays claim to those who are His subjects; as "Shepherd" Christ maintains a watchful eye over each and all who are members of His fold.

He is our Shepherd King, and His Lordship can only be measured to its depth in terms of His mercy and love for the likes of us—we are *His people, the sheep of His pasture!* When the people of Israel felt that they'd been lost to God, this is what the Lord said through the voice of His prophet Ezekiel:

> See, I Myself will search for My flock and look for them. As a shepherd looks for his sheep on the day he is among his scattered flock, so I will look for My flock. I will rescue them from all the places where they have been scattered . . . I will bring them out from the peoples . . . and bring them into their own land . . . I will tend them with good pasture . . . I will tend My flock and let them lie down . . . I will seek the lost, bring back the strays, bandage the injured, and strengthen the weak. (Ezekiel 34:11–16)

In His promise as proclamation is His Word, in His Word is His presence, and in His presence we are embraced in, enfolded by, an eternal love. These are the trusted words of our Shepherd King;

this is the promise that'll never fail us; and this "love Divine, all loves excelling" is the foundation of our expression of love for our Christ in this Lenten season. Amen.

Two

1 Corinthians 1:4–9

Nothing is Lacking

I always thank my God for you because of God's grace given to you in Christ Jesus, that by Him you were enriched in everything—in all speech and knowledge. In this way, the testimony about Christ was confirmed among you, so that you do not lack any spiritual gift as you eagerly wait for the revelation of our Lord Jesus Christ. He will strengthen you to the end, so that you will be blameless in the day of our Lord Jesus Christ. God is faithful; you were called by Him into fellowship with His Son, Jesus Christ our Lord.

ON THIS, THE FIRST of four Sundays marking the holy season of *Advent*, it's more than fitting that we should focus on, what has been called, by a variety of descriptions, the Second Coming of Christ, the return of Christ—or more frequently in Christian tradition—the Second Advent of Christ. This morning we join Christians throughout the world and the Church catholic in a remembrance of the first advent of Christ as the basis for our conviction that Christ will also one day return. This is not to join those

1 Corinthians 1:4-9

who foolishly speculate concerning the day and hour of Christ's return or the second coming of Christ at the end of time. As was said by Jesus Christ in our Gospel lesson, "Now concerning that day or hour no one knows—neither the angels in heaven nor the Son—except the Father." (Mk. 13:32)

This form of biblical genre is found throughout the Old Testament—for example in the *Book of Daniel* or in the *Book of Ezekiel*—and is common in the New Testament as well. Found spread all throughout the gospels, the Greek term for this "end time" narrative is *apokalypsis*; it means to unveil or to disclose a secret or mystery of God that was formally hidden from human consciousness of historical realities; in a more general sense to share a thing formally unknown that bears directly on the spiritual welfare of those in the covenant-community and in the wider world. Speaking in the most general terms, as a genre in the scriptures, *apokalysis* is a heavenly vision having to do with earthly realities. The "end" disclosed, while associated with a terminal end, is more often intended to convey the fulfillment of God's plan of salvation within history, from above history, which is a more accurate translation of the Greek term for "end," which is *telos*. The vision of the "end" or "fulfillment" is often conveyed through a *mediator*, called a "seer," shared with members of the faith community. And this revelation, always relevant to the present realities of God's people, if not the wider world, discloses some aspect of God's plan of redemptive history.

As given, the revelation always includes two related realms of history; the one temporal and the other spatial. God provides a vision about the future, but always and only as it relates to both past and present; that's the temporal aspect. There's also and always a connection made between things of heaven and the realities of earth; that's the spatial piece. Why is that important? Because so often those who talk about such passages in the Bible tend to make all of the related symbolism sound bizarre, unrelated to daily realities of life and living; or they make it sound unearthly. Even worse are those interpretations of this genre that force its symbolism to conform to the events of history, either present or projected into the future, and with such dire consequences that one can only respond with dread and horror at the mere prospect of such an event.

But this form of literature was never meant to strike fear in the hearts of God's own people; nor was it ever intended to sound fatalistic and foreboding. I'm only too aware that there are a whole host of television or radio personalities who've misused the apocalyptic passages in Scripture in a way that's disconcerting to some and downright frightening to others. That's not what this form of biblical story was intended to elicit in God's people; I assure you! Rather, we should think of apocalyptic stories as the biblical affirmation of a far more gracious and loving God, a Lord who will not abandon His plan for the redemption of humanity and the restoration of the cosmic order to circumvent the destructive intent of the "principalities and powers." This genre speaks as clearly to the faithfulness and love of God as does any passage from the less obscure portions of Scripture; genuine hope is at the heart of the apocalyptic imagery!

In this form of disclosure God is, in essence, revealing to His own people, and through them to the world, that regardless of how rigorous life gets, how frequently wars ravage the face of the earth, how uncertain we feel about tomorrow—He is with us now, as He's been in the past, and as He will be in the future. With Mark's account we're given the wonderful assurance that God's hand can and will be seen to have directed the course of the whole of history — past, present, and future. God is there to guide His own creation and covenant-creature through any and every time of suffering to reach His far greater, benevolent, goal.

There's enough suffering, sorrow, sickness, brutality, and a whole host of humanly caused injustices in this world, without having to be concerned with a future in which God is said to initiate some cataclysmic horror. I much prefer Mark's image of the future realities (see, Mk. 13:27!), in which the disclosure of the power and glory of Christ will involve a *homecoming* of sorts for all the saints of God—living and dead. Like you, I've seen enough of human suffering in my lifetime, so that this story, as told by Mark,

1 Corinthians 1:4–9

is a welcome breath of hopeful fresh air. I tire of hearing those who would prepare us for the coming of Christ by issuing a stern warning that in the end we might not measure-up to the standards *they've* set, and so be excluded from the joy of God's Kingdom! And many of those who issue such stern warning are embedded in the theology of the Reformers, so that one has to wonder: What have they done with the Pauline doctrine of justification by grace through faith? Granted, we are all, each of us, accountable to our Lord for the use or misuse of the spiritual gifts we've been given for ministry in His name and to God's greater glory, or for our inattention to the tasks of ministry to which He has called us. But to erroneously paint such a grim picture of the finality to God's plan of salvation will not awaken the lethargic to a more faithful and devoted service to the Savior.

Mark's account of the return of Christ will have none of that stern and foreboding stuff. It's a message of grace and of hope for human hearts in pain. *For all* who have come to believe that, even as a Christian, they'll somehow be excluded in the end. *For all* who wonder if they've met the necessary criteria for inclusion in God's coming kingdom of love, peace, harmony, and reunion with loved ones and friends. *For all* who question the firmness of their faith, the constancy of their devotion, or the certainty of their salvation in Jesus, Mark offers this spectacular account of a final *homecoming* for all of God's saints. The angels of God are sent to claim all who are His own and to bring them home, at last, to a love that'll never end. This marvelous account of Christ's Second Advent will only make sense to those who recognize the intent and purpose of God in Christ's First Advent into this world.

This wonderful narrative, as we have been given it in Mark's gospel, is the only assurance we need that all who're in Christ—all who've gone before us in this life and all who're yet with us—will one Day experience a grand and glorious *homecoming* and the establishment of God's kingdom in all the earth. And on this, another First Sunday in Advent, we're to remember that the One who took on human flesh, who bore our sins to the cross of Calvary, and who was resurrected and lives to reign and return for His own, is the same Savior—past, present, and future, or as is said by the author of *Hebrews*: "Jesus Christ is the same, yesterday, today, and forever!" (Hebrews 13:8) That same future *homecoming* becomes our present reality each and every time we gather at the Table of Jesus Christ, to know Him in the *bread that is broken* and in the *cup that is poured-out*. At this Table we are one family-of-family—brothers and sisters in the Lord—with the Church catholic, in time and beyond time, in place and beyond place. This Feast of a Future fulfillment making Present, to and for us here and now, the One who's promised to bring His great-plan-of-salvation to completion in a coming Kingdom of Grace, is appropriately celebrated on this First Sunday in Advent.

This *eucharistic* meal, this *feast* of the simplest of elements known on earth—bread and wine—is intended to provoke the remembrance of Who it is we trust, and how it is that He loves us, and why it is that we have hope of His return. Why bother ourselves with meaningless speculations, when we have before us this morning the sacramental celebration of a Redeemer whose love is forever, whose care is ceaseless, whose promise and Real Presence is the measure of our security in this world and the next. The fact that we remember *Him* is essential to our faith and hope for the future; but the fact that He remembers *us* is the substance of our hope in salvation and the reason for our rejoicing. In Jesus our Savior, in this sacramental meal, in the fellowship we share in the Spirit of Christ—*nothing is lacking*! It's only and always in the Presence of Christ that we receive a foretaste of all the fullness of God as grace, mercy, forgiveness—and hope.

Here's how Paul affirmed the truth of Mark's account as well as the true essence of this sacramental meal:

> He will strengthen you to the end, so that you will be blameless in the day of our Lord Jesus Christ. God is faithful; you were called by Him into fellowship with His Son, Jesus Christ our Lord. (1 Cor. 1:8–9) Amen.

Three

Philippians 2:5–11
The Admirable Exchange

Make your own attitude that of Christ Jesus, who existing in the form of God, did not consider equality with God as something to be used to His own advantage.
Instead He emptied Himself by assuming the form of a slave, taking on the likeness of men . . . And . . . He humbled Himself by becoming obedient to the point of death—even to death on a cross.

THE WORDS ARE THOSE of the Apostle Paul from his letter to the Philippians. They're thought to be the lyric to an early Christian hymn to Christ; and in particular to Christ in His humility and in His exaltation by God. If a hymn, like our own sacred songs, this lyrical language portrays—in such a strikingly dramatic fashion—the whole of the life of Christ in but a few concise verses! And like the hymnody with which you and I are so familiar, those great hymns we can sing from memory and with gusto, perhaps one can imagine this piece of sacred lyric resonating throughout the catacombs of Rome, sung by Christians whose worship needed to be hidden away to avoid murderous persecution. As a lyric it contains the fundamental conviction of the Christian community: Service to a Savior whose humility is the hallmark of His being, to be emulated by those who would follow His lead, and whose Beauty is bound-up in the brokenness associated with the burden of salvation from sin. Later in the theology of church this same lyric became the basis for what was then called the "admirable exchange."

Christ left the glory of His heavenly abode to become the incarnate Lord and Savior. The passion of our Lord does not begin with the events of Holy Week, but from the exact moment He determined, in full devotion to the will of His Father, to forsake all of the glory of His Father's presence for the salvation of humankind and the redemption of the whole of the cosmic order. With the incarnation of Christ—His becoming one with the whole of humanity—His entering into the full measure of all human existence, yet without sin—we became the beneficiaries of such grace and mercy as could only have come from the heart of God. Christ came to exchange all that was devastated by sin, all that was darkened by death, all that was lost by human disobedience, with the mercy of divine forgiveness, the hope of eternal life, the spiritual empowerment to overcome temptation, and eventual conferral of the Spirit upon those He would call His *ecclesia*—His Church. All of this glorious exchange had its beginnings in the singular act of humility in and from the heart of Christ.

This drama of our salvation was referred to as the admirable exchange because it was an act of God; in all that Christ brought to our broken and battered existence, we were the recipients of unmerited favor, acceptance, and love. It was admirable because it was a gift of grace beyond all comprehension, and it was admirable because it brought us all the beauty of heaven, renewing the face and inner force of all creation as foretaste of a future fulfillment. It was called the admirable exchange because the gifts of God's grace received far exceeded the depravation and disgrace of human sin; what was merited was judgment, what was exchanged was Christ taking the judgment for our sins on Himself; what was merited

Philippians 2:5–11

was rejection, what was exchanged was Christ receiving us and making reconciliation with God our reality; what was merited was death, what was exchanged was the gift of eternal life in Christ risen, reigning, and returning.

In the 1970's Christian novelist, Walter Wangrin, wrote a short piece entitled, *Ragman*; a story intended to dramatize the concept of the admirable exchange with imagery startlingly contemporary and profoundly gripping.

Perhaps intended to be imaginative, or the recounting of a genuine experience, the story opens with the narrator recounting to a child his once having noticed a young man, handsome and strong, walking the alleys of their city, pulling what appeared to be an old cart filled with clothes. The clothing was both bright and new, and the young man pulling the cart cried out: "Rags! New rags for old! I take your tired rags!"

As the narrator goes on, he tells of the "ragman's" exchanging a grieving woman's hanky with a linen cloth "so clean and nice that it shined." On leaving the woman, the "ragman" placed her hanky to his own face, and he began to weep her tears. Next he encounters a young girl whose head is bleeding and wrapped in a bandage; the "ragman" exchanges her bloody bandage for a lovely yellow bonnet. As he walked away, he placed the bandage on his own head, and both her wound and bleeding became his own! Finally, the "ragman" came upon a man whose right arm had been lost in the war; he was homeless and lost. The "ragman" took the vets field-jacket and exchanged it with his own glorious coat—and the vet's former disability became the "ragman's" in return.

Finally, the narrator says, the ragman "climbed a hill. With tormented labor he cleared a little space on that hill. Then he sighed. He lay down. He pillowed his head on a hanky and a field-jacket. He covered his bones with a blanket. And he died."

All that was ruinous, all that was broken, all that was bent toward death, all exchanged for the glorious gifts of a loving and benevolent God. But, even as our own glorious gospel would have it, the ragman was resurrected on Sunday morning, with "no sign of sorrow or of age and all the rags shined for cleanness." In this imaginative story, the *admirable exchange* was completed—as it was in the resurrected and reigning Christ—at least from the side of our God; which begs the question: What is there from *our* side in light of this admirable exchange?

Maybe the action taken by the narrator of this story can be replicated in our own lives—and on this evening of all evenings. He testifies to what followed, saying: "Well, then I lowered my head and trembling for all that I had seen, I myself walked up to the Ragman. I told him my name with shame, for I was a sorry figure next to him. Then I took off my clothes in that place, and I said to him with dear yearning in my voice: 'Dress me.' He dressed me. My Lord, he put new rags on me, and I am a wonder beside him."

Isn't that a remarkable statement: "Dress me!" What more could be confessed by the disciple of Christ than to be "dressed" in the garments of His gracious humility and His deepest devotion to the will and way of God the Father? The garments of grace may not be esteemed of much value in a culture fascinated with the garish and obscene, and yet they are radiant with the glory of the Redeemer. We should make no other request, save that which is so profoundly expressed by the character in this story: "Dress me."

This evening (Christmas Eve) is glorious for any number of reasons, all of them somewhat shrouded in the mystery that rightly belongs to all things sacred. Yet on this eve of Christmas, the concept of the admirable exchange is paramount! Without the event of this exchange there would have been no virginal conception, no infant born in a manger, no visitation by shepherds and later by magi, nothing for us to celebrate and no reason for us to be here this evening, or on any other occasion for that matter. This exchange is the singular event in the history of humankind that brought about a seismic shift of all things in the direction of reconciliation, restoration, and renewal; this exchange, first whispered in the hallways of heaven as a mere rumor, only to explode onto the stage of history with the cry of a shivering infant—this exchange is the beginning and the end (as goal) of "the greatest story ever told." It's this story that tells us who *He* is and who *we* are in Him and under the power of His Holy Spirit.

Philippians 2:5-11

    Go to the manger in the chill of night and touch with your finger the cheek of the Son of God, made flesh in infant life; go to the manger in the black of night, surrounded by the lowest of the lowly, and hear an infant voice whimper, knowing how that same voice will one day herald the Gospel of our salvation; go to the manger and lay your longing eyes on the form of Him who is King of kings and Lord of lords, and yet "emptied Himself, by assuming the form of a slave, taking on the likeness of (human flesh)" (Phil. 2:7). Amen.

Four

Luke 2:1–14
Holiness in Human Flesh

In that region there were shepherds living in the fields, keeping watch over their flock by night. Then an angel of the Lord stood before them, and the glory of the Lord shone around them, and they were terrified. . . ..And suddenly there was with the angel a multitude of the heavenly host, praising God and saying,
  "Glory to God in the highest heaven,
  and on earth peace among those
  whom he favors!"

 They are such powerful words, and in particular in our world where all things *holy* seem to have vanished; there is much that is mundane, common, of the earth—but too little of that which the Bible calls *holy*; in the simplest of terms the word *holy* represents anything that has been *set apart for service to God*. So that angels are said to be *holy*, or those who gave the entirety of their lives in love of God, and in the desire to devote the total of life to God's will, are said to have been *holy*; or in what is its most general and popular usage of the term, the Bible itself is said to be a *holy* book.
 Yet, for our contemporaries—and maybe even for some of us in this sanctuary—there's nothing exceptional about this day

Luke 2:1–14

(Christmas day). Oh, there're those things that touch the heart and make this one day somewhat special, like the presence of family, or the gleam in the eyes of children, or the smell of Christmas cookies and a beautifully decorated tree. But beyond those things, is there anything in our sense of expectation which we might see, hear, or feel, to justify the claim to make this one day *holy*?

Part of the problem we face is that the word–*holy*–has fallen into disuse; to prove the point, all you need do is ask yourself how often you've used the word *holy* in a sentence in, say, the last week or two. Maybe the only time we hear the word spoken anymore is when we come to church on Sunday mornings, when it appears to have been pulled from the shelf of obscure liturgical language, dusted off, and dropped into the liturgy just in case we forget its importance. Nevertheless, on this one day of the year, we let the word pass over our lips, whether in song or in prayer, without so much as a twinge at the terrifying nature of the word as intended by the whole of Scripture and even in much of Christian tradition.

Rudolf Otto once wrote that the presence of the *holy* is *mysteriosum facinans et tremendum*; the transcendent, the mysterious, that which is otherwise unapproachable; and yet, that to which the human soul and spirit seem irresistibly drawn—like a moth to the flame. He was attempting to put all practitioners of Christian faith on notice that the very thing to which we are drawn, out of sheer fascination, is also the reality that can cause us to feel a deep and unspeakable sense of reverent awe. Recall what was said of the shepherds in Luke's account, when the angel of the Lord appeared to them and the glory of the Lord shone round about them; they were—what? Filled with terror, with fear; that is *mysteriosum facinans et tremendum*.

We come into this sacred space in the hope of having some contact with God, and chance a meeting with a *mystery* that is both terrifying in holiness and judgment, yet tender in love and mercy. The babe wrapped in swaddling clothes, lying in a manger, is about as subtle as a tsunami. And those who first felt the winds of that coming storm, like shepherds and others, were wise enough to know that whenever you come into the presence of the

The Gospel of Grace for Wounded Sojourners

Holy–the only safe place to be is on your knees. There're few scenes more often artistically depicted on Christmas cards than is that manger scene with the *holy* family reverently placed beside the manger wherein rests the Son of God incarnate, and shepherds kneeling in worship adoration. This form of representation captures, in a wonderful way, the striking contrast—the paradox—of this singular revelatory event: there in the commonality of a stable, housing as it does the most ordinary of earth's creatures, including the human presence, resides the Redeemer of humankind, the Holy-of-Holies in human form. This infant, who breathes into His tiny lungs the rancid air of his nursery, breathes out the blessed air of a *holy* benediction!

Yes, it was a little babe in a makeshift basinet; yet they knew this infant-Savior had His origins in the heart of a *holy* God. Like those strangers from the Far East who would come sometime later to visit this child, the shepherds attended to the stable in order to pay homage to *holiness* incarnate. Of all days, *this* day is said to be *holy*, because—and only because—the One whose birth we've come here to celebrate was the *holiness* of the Lord housed in the humble-nature of our common humanity. We're given such a glorious message on this Christmas day, a message that's repeated each year only because humankind will never weary of receiving this redemptive Word, which alone brings healing to wounded hearts and souls. It is a living reminder to us all that even in the midst of our most common affairs, perhaps there more than all other environments, something of the sacred, the *holy*, breaks through and blesses us—this Christ comes to us, dripping of a divine holiness, and dowses us in the grace of God. Christmas—the infant Christ in His feeding trough—is that dramatic image with which we are so richly blessed, because it is a token of just how it is that a *holy* God has laid-hold of our most lowly human condition, lifting our humanity to the heights of heaven above! Christmas day is the hallmark of that *holy* event in which a humanity made ugly by sin was transformed through the tender life of the Infant born in Bethlehem, and re-created with a beauty bearing all the glory its limited form can contain.

Luke 2:1–14

So, if we hope to encounter the *holy* this day, maybe we should start by staring into the face of the person in the pew beside us; or perhaps we should set-out from here and visit some lonely soul who has no one else to care; or stop-by an emergency room and see if there isn't someone in need of a hand to hold; or tend to the neighbor who's celebrating her first Christmas in the absence of her husband of forty-seven years. As disciples of Christ, and in the power of the Spirit, we too can bring the glow of the *holy* into those situations that are desolate of all delight, and to those poor souls who—for whatever reasons—seem to have forgotten that there's a God whose love for them is unmatched and who desires to deliver them from sin and death. By our very presence—as prayerful Christian presence—we can demonstrate the profound delight that comes from the conviction that there is a dimension to life that is genuinely *holy*—set-apart for God—and how embracing that holiness opens the floodgates of faith to communion with Christ, His Son.

The story is told of the child who went to mid-night Christmas service with her mother; when the time came for communion, the little girl yanked on her mother's coat sleeve and asked in a voice choked with excitement and joyful expectation, "Is this the time when Christ comes down from heaven?" I'd say that child had a keen sense of what it is to come into the presence of the *holy*. And maybe this one day, this one most special day, you and I will experience a taste of that same excitement and joyful expectation. After all, this *is* the day "when Christ came down from heaven," isn't it? Amen.

Five

Mark 15:16–32

Haunted by the Cross of Christ

"Soldiers took Jesus, and they led Him away... they took Jesus, and they led Him away...they led Him away, to die on a Cross of shame." The words form a portion of the lyric from the anthem selected for worship this (Maundy Thursday) evening; actually, they're applicable for any time in the Lenten season, in particular, the constant refrain "They led Him away."

This poignant anthem refers to the mood of that somber day on which a cross was raised on a desolate hill just outside the walls of the holy city of Jerusalem. It is a hill "far away;" clearly removed from us—geographically and historically. Yet the cross raised on that same hill has cast a long shadow over all, haunting human history, leaving its mark on the human conscience and its image etched on the human soul. Golgotha; a dark, desolate place, associated with cruelty and injustice, has now—providentially—become the place of the world's salvation:

> There is a green hill far away,
> Without a city wall,

Mark 15:16–32

Where the dear Lord was crucified,
Who died to save us all.

The cross of Christ has held the fascination of the human imagination ever since the gloomy day when it was raised-up on the rocky heights of Golgotha's stony facade. It has inspired hymnists, playwrights, and painters, the pious as well as the profane, storytellers and song writers, like the lyricist for this evening's anthem.

In the 1940's, during the terror of Nazi Germany, there was a young pastor by the name of Dietrich Bonhoeffer, martyred before celebrating his fortieth birthday; hung from a make-shift scaffold by the Gestapo for having participated in one of several attempts to assassinate Hitler. In one of his numerous theological reflections, this profoundly insightful theologian wrote: "The cross is God's truth about us, and therefore it is the only power which can make us truthful. When we know the cross we are no longer afraid of the truth." If we can grasp Pastor Bonhoeffer's profoundly insightful observation—as I believe we can and must—we'll be given an insight into one of the more urgent meanings of the cross of Christ and the season of Lent. Surprisingly, we're at the same time afforded a window through which we can better see the relationship between the lyric of our anthem for this evening, this sermonic reflection, and the observance of the Lenten season.

I see a parallel between Bonhoeffer's remark that the cross of Christ is "God's truth about us," so that when we come to know the cross "we are no longer afraid of the truth," and that portion of the lyric of this evening's anthem which reads: "Christ cried out in pain. Father, please forgive them. They know not what they do." Both—in parallel—disclose one of the principal lessons to be learned in our observation of this most holy season: As those who are haunted by the cross of Christ, we can be honest and face the truth about ourselves; we find that our observation of this Lenten season is faithful only in the practice of genuine repentance. Haunted by the cross of Christ, we discover it much easier to be honest and face the truth about ourselves, remaining attentive to the echoes of sins, formerly committed, for which we need forgiveness and the guilt from which we desire to be released.

The renowned reformer, John Calvin, said of Christ's cross that his death was sufficient for all: it was efficient for many. That is to say, the cross of Christ, constructed of God's love—in the language of the letter of First Peter—covers a multitude of sins—for all people. Yet only those who have claimed faith in Christ as Lord and Savior will comprehend how efficient the cross of Christ is in eradicating the consequences of sin from the human heart, soul, mind, self.

It was not uncommon for poets in the Middle Ages to suggest that love governed God in offering the gift of forgiveness in the cross of Christ. As he contemplated the cross of Christ, one of the Greek theologians of the early church spoke of God as the sweet overlord; offering salvation to those who were undeserving. There were no cords that could hold Christ's arms to the cross-beam, and no nails that could fix him to the wood of the cross; the love of God alone held Christ fast to the cross, bearing the misery of our sin. The truth we are compelled to see in Christ's cross is our complete incapacity to address the consequences of sin, even through our own best efforts. We were held prisoner to the consequences of sin as surely as a prisoner is confined by his or her cell.

Lent is the season in which we come to the remembrance that our redemption—that is to say, our freedom from the consequences of sin—was gained for us by the suffering of our Lord's passion; again and from our anthem: "Christ cried out in pain. Father, please forgive them." In this season of searching our own hearts, souls, and minds—willing captives to the cross of Christ—we face the echoes of sins, both of commission and omission; those sins we have tended to avoid in even our most generous confession.

Echoes of sin reverberate in our hearts and minds as candidly, and sometimes as abrasively, as did those of the crowd all clamoring for the release of Barabbas and the crucifixion of Christ; we stand accused by a cruel and unsympathetic judgment no less unjust then the horrific accusations flung at Christ as He hung from the gallows. Echoes of sin can be deeply unsettling, as they

Mark 15:16-32

whisper into our souls, some sin we have committed, but always in an accusatory key, lacking insight, mercy, grace, and forgiveness. Echoes of former sins continue to resound within the walls of our heart, long after the time when first committed; they haunt us with a truth we've been reluctant to face, even more—unwilling to admit and confess; they haunt us as surely as we are haunted by the shadow of our Savior's cross.

But Lent is the glorious season of grace when we Christians are showered with the greater truth of our God's towering love, a love exceeding even our gravest sin and the rumblings long left behind. Lent is the season in which we can be washed clean in the power of God's Spirit, as we face our failures in faith and look to the Crucified Christ for forgiveness and the inner strength to seek His way once again. Lent is the season in which we receive the *echo* of yet another Word; the good news that will calm all fears and dispel apprehension that our offences have caused our God to disown us: "Father, please forgive them. They know not what they do!"

We do well to receive the echo of the voice of Peter Lewis when he writes: "At Calvary we see what sin deserves and what God requires. Calvary was too terrible to be optional, the suffering involved too enormous to be unnecessary, and the Sufferer too precious to his Father to have been given over needlessly to such pain." In this season of Lent, with the ears to listen, we'll hear the echoes of forgiveness drowning-out the murmur of a guilty conscience; and that, solely by the grace and mercy to be found in the Cross of Christ.

In the powerful words of St. Thomas a Kempis: "There is no health of soul, nor hope of eternal life, except in the cross" (of Christ); words we want to remember, and in particular as we join others in the observation of this most holy week of Christ's passion. Amen.

Six

John 20:24–25

"Setting the Record Straight"

But one of the Twelve, Thomas (called the "Twin"), was not with them when Jesus came. So the other disciples kept telling him, "We have seen the Lord!"

So, IF ONLY FOR this morning, let's set the record straight. The disciple, Thomas, was not so much in doubt as he was in pain. In fact, he was caught in the clenched jaws of a crisis and trial. His beloved Teacher and Master had been nailed to a Roman cross, like a common criminal. With each last, long, and labored breath Jesus took on the scaffold, I'm certain Thomas heard the promised day of deliverance dying as well. Christian novelist, Frederick Buechner, writes that whenever we feel as though life has collapsed, or whenever our tiny human frames groan under the weight of hardship and heart-ache, our view of life in general can become increasingly pessimistic. He writes: "It's all we can do just to keep our heads above water. So we dig a hole in the ground, in ourselves, in our bustling about, or wherever else we dig it, and hide the terrible

John 20:24-25

things in it, which is another way of saying that we hide ourselves from the terrible things."

That's true, isn't it? Isn't that exactly what we do whenever our dreams look like they might turn to dust? Don't we wish, hope, and long for some place to hide from the pain and uncertainty of situations beyond our control and crushing-in on us on all sides? Thomas suffered the death of Jesus. I can only imagine how in that tragic event Thomas thought he was watching the dismantling of his entire world. Where in the world do you go for comfort when a cross up-and-swallows the *one* source of strength you were *certain* would never be overcome? And where do you turn when your shoulders bend beneath the weight of a sorrow or emotional burden so heavy, you feel as though you'll one day soon break apart? Where do we find solace in situations of heartfelt despair?

I believe it's always by the grace of God, and in the power of the Holy Spirit that we're upheld, whenever our faith grows faint and our soul gets all tangled-up in some terrible disappointment and doubt. Because God knows what we need, when we need it, and exactly where we need to be to receive it. It's certainly not some twist of fate, or mere accident of timing that Thomas was gifted with the grace of Christ's presence in the midst of his fellow believers, you know. I'm sure that the gospel writer wants us to get the message. If we want Christ, we'd best begin by looking to the fellowship of the faithful in the worshipping and serving congregation of His church.

That's what makes our worship so essential to our faith; it's not primarily about what we have to bring to God. It's actually about what *God* will bring to *us* in the context of *this* prayer, *that* hymn, or some informal conversation with another believer following worship. This Easter Sunday gathering, in this sanctuary, is about God's gift of the Holy Spirit. It's about our need to be reminded how we're a people being saved and made saintly, by the power and in the presence of our crucified and risen Lord Christ. It's about the One who comes to us in the spoken Word of worship, wrapping His grace around our lives.

The Gospel of Grace for Wounded Sojourners

Look again at the experience of Thomas and the other disciples of Jesus; look at what they received when, at last, as Christ stood in the midst of their misery and as the Risen Savior. Essentially Jesus said something like: "I forgive you for your failures of faith in me; you remain my friends; come and continue to follow me in the power of my Holy Spirit." That's what we call unconditional, unexpected, irresistible grace! And stunned to silence by such grace, Thomas fell flat on his face in worship and adoration.

After all, Jesus already knew about the demand Thomas had placed, or the condition for personal belief he placed before the others, when he said brazenly: "If I don't see the mark of the nails in His hands, put my finger into the mark of the nails, and put my hand into His side, I will never believe!" You remember when Jesus met Thomas face-to-face; what was the first thing he said to him? He said, "Put your finger here and observe My hands. Reach out your hand and put it into My side. Don't be an unbeliever, but a believer." That would've been a deeply unsettling experience for Thomas. Because it meant that Jesus had heard *every single word* of the demand Thomas had made! That could be a valuable lesson for any one of us, the next time we think to speak an unkind word, or issue thoughtless criticism of another, or spread some malicious gossip. Wouldn't it make a difference, if before we did we thought to ourselves, "Oh, that's right, Christ will also hear this?"

But here's the grace: Jesus didn't chide, correct, or chastise Thomas for such a foolish and faithless demand. Jesus extended pure grace, as if to say, "Thomas, if that's what you need for the establishment of faith, well, here it is!" That's the gospel's way of affirming that the Lord made himself manifest to Thomas as an act of ultimate acceptance and confirming love. In that simple act, Jesus graced Thomas with forgiveness, as he had the others in ways they needed as well. Christ also comes to us with love and acceptance.

Seeing the risen Christ was all those first followers needed to once again find faith. It must've been such a powerful and gripping experience; it dissolved all doubt and fear, and washed away their guilt for having abandoned Jesus in his hour of greatest need.

John 20:24-25

As a consequence, those who were cowering one day, were motivated by a spiritual courage that would willingly take-on even the whole of the Roman empire. They received a vision of the risen Lord Christ, because without that encounter, the gospel would've seemed nothing more than another tragic tale. But the gospel was born in the womb of witness to the resurrected Christ, given by the first followers; and perhaps it's that witness which brings us here this morning or every Sunday morning. Yet for me, the most captivating aspect of this appearance narrative in John's Gospel, is when Jesus says to Thomas and all of his disciples: "Those who believe without seeing are blessed."

At that point in the story, I imagine Jesus peering over the shoulders of the disciples, and locking his eyes on you and me. These words are meant for you, for me, for us together. These words are intended for those who continue to gather, care, seek, serve, and worship each and every Lord's Day, long after the glow of Easter has given way to the gritty and often unrecognized work of cross-bearing-discipleship on a daily basis. We each of us are blessed because we were not in that room on the evening of the first Easter day; nor were we in the same place eight-days-later when Thomas received the wonderful vision of the risen Lord Christ.

We are blessed simply because we've believed a *witness* to God's triumph in the risen Christ; a witness who was pastor, parent, Sunday school teacher, or friend to us. We're blessed because we're here this morning offering our lives to the Lord we can't even see. Jesus is mindful of our situation; he knows how hard it can be, and often is, to keep faith when others fall away. Jesus is aware of our efforts to overcome some failure or misconduct.

In this story we're told that for all who would follow those first disciples, God's blessings would come in listening to the *same* Lord, loving in the *same* Spirit, sacrificing for the *same* service, and forgiving with the *same* faithfulness. In point of fact, it's because faith and following can be so very difficult in the absence of some demonstrable evidence of Christ's presence that you and I are blessed. Jesus commends us *because* we believe in his power, promise, and presence by hearing and not by sight. We've been blessed of God because we attempt to carry forward the faith of the apostles on the basis of having heard the good news, which is exactly what Peter told some Christians removed from Christ's resurrection by one whole generation: "You love Him, though you have not seen Him. And though not seeing Him now, you believe in Him and rejoice with inexpressible and glorious joy, because you are receiving the goal of your faith, the salvation of your souls" (1 Peter 1:8–9). How do we believe in the real presence of Christ, when for all intents and purposes, the world looks like it's going to hell in a hand basket?

Well Jesus said it and we can drink it in, like water from a fountain of refreshment in a dry and weary land: "Those who believe without seeing are blessed." It's all about the power of the Word and our willingness to hear and believe that Word. In other words, faith is born at the ear and not at the eye. The grace of God comes to touch and transform our lives, more in *sound* than in it does in *sight;* or perhaps better said: faith in Christ comes in a sacred-sound giving birth to faithful sight. We might not *see* Christ, but he *sees* us.

Christ sees you and me and us together. He sees us just as he saw Thomas: our failures, struggles, deep and paralyzing fears; our feelings of inadequacy and efforts to overcome some nasty character traits. Christ sees our wounds and worries, our problems and pains. He sees us, each of us, each day, every day, doing our level best to shoulder that cross of sacrificial service.

Christ knows how desperately we hunger for his word, are needful of his love, and yearn for his forgiveness. Christ comes to us as he once did Thomas, to heal our wounded hearts, to break the chains of a critical spirit, to breathe energy into our exhausted faith. He comes to us in Word and Spirit to bless our souls, to bend our wills to his own; he comes to see, to soothe, and to save.

Amen.

Seven

John 20:27-28

Rejoicing in the Wounds of Christ

Then (Jesus) said to Thomas, "Put your finger here and observe my hands. Reach out your hand and put it into my side. Don't be an unbeliever, but a believer." Thomas responded to Him, "My Lord and my God!"

PERHAPS THIS ACCOUNT OF the encounter between Thomas and the risen Christ is *too* familiar; there is, of course, the tendency for us to all too quickly pass-over that which is familiar—missing the subtlety and shades of significance in the all-too familiar story. Here's just one example of what I mean: Notice that the gospel writer doesn't tell us how Thomas reacted to the command of Christ; we're not told if he actually felt the nail-marks on the wrists of Christ and thrust his hand into the gaping wound at His side. John leaves that to our imaginations; or what is more correct, John wants us to recall how it is that when Christ commands anything of those who follow—there are only two options—obey or disobey the command. In other words, Thomas must've reached-out his hand to touch the wounds of Christ as his Master commanded him to do, or how are we to make sense of his response, in that vivid exclamation: "My Lord and my God."

I must admit that I had never before considered the fact that Thomas had to reach-out his hand and touch the open wounds of Christ. And I never before considered what it must've been like to affirm the suffering and death of his Master—not by eye-witness account *only*, but by the jagged edge of nail-print and spear wound felt with his own hand. It seems to give to faith an investment in the physical reality of what our Lord suffered. Beyond that, this is the one account where we are given evidence of another striking confirmation; the risen and glorified body of Christ also bears, for all eternity, the wounds endured in the full measure of His suffering, for us and for our salvation. We cannot have the risen, glorified, and reigning Lord Christ, without at the same time witnessing on His own resurrected and living body the brutal wounds of His passion and death.

And should the question be raised: "Why would the Lord bear those terrible marks on His glorified body? Why did He not, rather, erase them from His risen body?" The answer is, I believe, quite simple—and yet deep—He chose to retain His passion scars on His glorified body as a reminder to us and not to Him. Not only as a reminder of His suffering for salvation, but just as importantly—as a visible reminder that this Lord personifies *all* pain! There's *no* suffering, *no* tragic event, *no* hardship, *no* injustice, *no* rejection, *no* pain, whether physical, emotional, or spiritual with which our Lord Christ does not (bear as His own)—helping us bear-up under the burden of such aching of the heart and soul. And yes, if it be His divine will, He also can and will not only empower us to endure—but to truly overcome such adversity! That knowledge, in and of itself, is sufficient for us to glory—and even rejoice—in the wounds of our Christ. But there is more to this story than that—there is *always* more to the gospel than any one particular theme or purpose in the telling.

Let me remind you that I find it inappropriate to call Thomas the "Doubter," as *doubt* was not at issue with him. Thomas was not unlike many contemporary Christians I've met. There was a

John 20:27-28

discrepancy—a somewhat glaring absurdity that forced Thomas to pose his challenge to the others who had *seen* the risen Christ; it wasn't so much that he doubted Christ had been resurrected, as he could not wrap his mind—as we would say today—around the fact that this *same* Jesus, the others claimed to have seen as risen from the dead, had been put-to-death on a Roman cross. The apostle Paul would, some years after this event, put the question of Thomas in the form of a confession; Paul wrote ". . . we preach Christ crucified, a stumbling block to the Jews and foolishness to the Gentiles."

And don't suppose that the others didn't struggle with the very same issue; in fact, in John's account, there's still some reservation on their part even after the risen Lord makes His appearance to them. But, Thomas? He needs to actually see *and* touch the wounds of the risen Christ in order to resolve this very real issue that stands, like a great granite wall, between him and his coming to faith in Jesus as the promised Messiah of God. And isn't it peculiar that Thomas expects to find that the risen Christ will bear the wounds of the cross on His glorified body? How could he have known, or why would he have even supposed, that Christ would still carry the marks of His crucifixion on His glorified body?

Here we encounter one of the great mysteries of the community of faith, disclosed in the relationship between Thomas and the others who have witnessed the risen Lord Christ. It's obviously the case that when the others testified to Thomas, they included mention of the wounds of Christ evident on His body. The community of faith—then as now—cannot bear testimony to any other risen Christ, save the One who still bears the scars of His passion on His risen and glorified body. In other words, bearing testimony to the wounds of the risen, reigning Christ is as essential to proclaiming the Gospel as is any other single characteristic of such testimony.

At this point Thomas is a symbol for all who will be followers of Christ in the future, in the sense that he can hear of, and have, no other Christ than the Lord whose passion will, for all eternity, be emblazoned on His hands, feet, and side. And the community of faith can bear testimony to no other Christ, save Him who as

Savior has taken the deepest and more desperate wound of sin into His own suffering, and by doing so, brought to fruitfulness the salvation of us all. Our Savior wears wounds. Yet He wears those same wounds as if they were jewels of great value; for indeed, they are, as they symbolize His willingness to demonstrate a love that looked squarely into the loveless situation of sin and its consequences, and transformed all who would welcome Him as their Lord and Savior.

The Holy Spirit has His own way of shaping the truth in the mouth of the disciple; the Spirit of God gifts us with truth we could not possibly have known by way of study, or intellect, or as a result of reasonable conclusion; the Holy Spirit discloses to the disciple the essential truth to be spoken in the manner in which God desires that same truth to be proclaimed. In the words of the *Letter to the Hebrews*: "Now faith is the reality of what is hoped for, the proof of what is not (yet) seen." Or, in the words of Christ: "Those who believe without seeing as blessed."

The point being that Thomas spoke the truth even *before* the truth was made clear to him. And in speaking that same word of truth, Thomas disclosed his faith—perhaps not yet as solid and well-formed as it was yet to become—but *faith* nonetheless. Yet there is an equally powerful image in these words of Thomas. His own testimony to the fact that the risen body of Christ would bear the wounds and scars of His passion and suffering is also, and at the same time, an expression of the only Christ Israel and the world would be given—a Christ whose glorified body will forever disclose the depth of God's love for the likes of us. God's love is ever greater than even our most egregious sin, greater than even the most entrenched heart, greater than death itself. Because the love of God took shape in the form of a crucified-Christ, we can forever take comfort in the knowledge that grace and mercy are unending for those who have placed faith and hope in Him.

Faith! When Thomas is engaged by the risen Christ, he must have fondled-in-faith those same suffered-wounds of Jesus; that is, in and of itself, an event almost too extraordinary to believe. But it is in the confession of Thomas that follows that we are given, what I have called, "reason to rejoice in the wounds of Christ." You'll

John 20:27-28

recall how Thomas exclaims: "My Lord and my God!" Nowhere in the whole of the New Testament, with the possible exception of one passage in *Romans*, is Jesus ever called *"God!"* Pre-or-post resurrection this is the only place where a disciple calls Jesus of Nazareth—*"God."* It's an affirmation that should take-our-breath-away; it should cause us to fall to our knees; it should give rise to astonishment; it is most assuredly a "reason to rejoice in Christ's wounds." We worship and adore no distant and removed deity, one who is aloof and unaffected by the afflictions and sufferings we are made to face in this life. This is the God who took into His own heart the consequences of our sinful rebellion and in all ways exchanged those same consequences for the fullness of grace, mercy, and forgiveness found in Christ Jesus. We rejoice in the wounds of the risen, reigning Christ because they are borne in the glorified body of the Son of God.

And these wounds are, therefore, now and for all eternity, as much a part of God's essence as is any other characteristic we would otherwise associate with His divine nature.

We rejoice in the wounds of Christ, as we are the Body of Christ and must bear all the world's wounds to the only place redemption is to be found—the grace and mercy of our crucified-God.

We rejoice in the wounds of Christ as our salvation. In point of fact, imagine that, while pointing to the wounded-form of the risen, reigning Jesus Christ, and in words attributed to the prophet Isaiah, Thomas were to proclaim to us: "Look, this is our God; we have waited for Him, and He has saved us. This is the LORD; we have waited for Him. Let us rejoice and be glad in His salvation!"Amen.

Eight

John 2:1–3

Celebrating a Kingdom

On the third day a wedding took place in Cana of Galilee. Jesus' mother was there, and Jesus and His disciples were invited to the wedding as well. When the wine ran out, Jesus mother told Him, "They don't have any wine."

IT MAKES PERFECT SENSE to focus on this particular story from John's gospel as our text for this morning's sermon, because we rightly associate the sacrament of infant baptism as well as wedding receptions as events to be celebrated. And this passage is about a wedding reception! But if we look deep within the theological intent of John's use of this story, we'll begin to appreciate just how vital John's narrative and its intended meaning are to our celebration of infant baptism as well.

First, it is only in John's gospel that we hear the story of the Passover meal, which includes an account of Jesus washing the feet of His disciples, and thereby giving witness to that form of love He commanded to be shared with each other and one another. Second, and perhaps of far greater importance to us this morning,

John 2:1–3

the account of Jesus at the wedding in Cana of Galilee—and all transpiring at that event— points to the most profound meaning of the coming kingdom of God, as an event of promise, hope, and joy of the kind only the Son of God could have made, and makes possible, for us.

I'll say what that same joy is and then elaborate: This is a story intended to disclose, in a singular fashion, the joy that is presently our own, and will be even more so as fulfillment, in the coming kingdom of God! It's an account of the way in which we can look to Jesus to enrich our lives, when all of those common props we use to support our life have failed—just as the wine failed at this wedding reception—or whenever we run short on what we perceive to be essential to fulfillment and joy in life. Whenever we have, quite unexpectedly, or because we have failed to plan adequately, found that we faced a certain kind of emptiness. Jesus is the essence of our personal fulfillment, and as the embodiment of God's coming kingdom He discloses the intent of God as one of gracious favor to us and to our children's children.

I'll say very little about the request that Mary makes of her Son, but only to point-out that her request is an obvious indication of her knowledge of the depth of her Son as the One who is undeniably compassionate and caring. Mary knows her Son to long for the fulfillment of those who experience emptiness, as One who desires to disclose the presence of God's reign even in the midst of a wounded world, and as the only One who can provide fulfillment on a level unparalleled by any other means. Such knowledge of her son is evident in one fact alone.

When Jesus says, "What has this concern of yours to do with me? My hour has not yet come;" Mary turns to the servants and says, simply, "Do whatever He tells you." In that one phrase Mary exhibits a keen sense of her Son's real character as the Christ: the One who can create fullness, bring renewal, call forth life out-of-death, and His word alone is sufficient.

And notice this: I wonder if Mary isn't looking over the shoulders of those servants, and locking her eyes on you and me, when she says, "Do whatever He tells you." In particular on this baptismal Sunday as we who have been baptized revisit our own vows and seek to become more faithful to the command of Christ, submitting to the empowerment of His Holy Spirit to place Christ-like "love" at the center of all we are and do in this life. I imagine that when Mary issues this word to us: "Do whatever He tells you," she would expect us to recall that the command we are to follow, to obey, is just this: "Love . . . as (Jesus) has loved you!" This tiny life that has now become a member of the body of Christ must be the object of our love—individually and communally—or we fail to be faithful to the charge we've been given in Christ.

Much has been made of the fact that Jesus tells the servants to fill six stone water jars, containing 20 to 30 gallons each, which totals 120 to 180 gallons that will soon become wine!

And rightly so; that is *more* than enough wine to keep several weddings in full supply—at least the wedding receptions I've attended. The image is one of extravagance, overabundance, more than could possibly be consumed by one small, rural, wedding party. The extravagance of God's grace made visible in the power of Christ's presence, even now, with us and for us, and of the even greater overabundance of joy and fulfillment to be anticipated in the coming kingdom of God—where none and nothing will lack!

The promise implicit in all of this is now given to John Robert and can never be taken from him as the singular act of God's grace and good will. This, the first of the signs, which is John's term for Christ's miracles, points to a Savior who seeks only our enrichment. What more could one possibly want for the life of this infant as he grows and matures in life, but that he will come to know the joy of such enrichment in Christ, and discover the fulfillment of all that has been given him on this morning. That is to say, that he is and always will be a child of God and a member of Christ's Church. And notice the remark of the steward in charge of the bar at this wedding in Cana of Galilee; he goes to the groom, and as if to complain, says, "Everyone sets out the fine wine first, then, after people have drunk freely, the inferior. But you have kept the fine wine until now."

John 2:1–3

Don't think the reference to fine wine simply a glowing affirmation of its quality—although it is that! This reference to fine wine recalls prophetic utterances referring to the coming kingdom of God. Think for example of that found in the prophet Amos. Speaking as all prophets do in the name of the Lord, Amos proclaimed how: "One day the mountains will drip with sweet wine, and all the hills will flow with it. I will restore the fortunes of My people Israel. . . They will plant vineyards and drink their wine!" The meaning wasn't lost on all who witnessed this *sign* of Jesus, and tasted this *fine wine*!

And neither should the meaning be lost on us on this baptismal Sunday morning—as we celebrate the gift of salvation to us and to our children—as we celebrate in the presence of that same Christ who brought new joy to the hearts of those at the wedding feast in Cana of Galilee, and provided for the fulfillment of all joy. God alone knows what personal experiences await (baptized child's name) as he grows and matures; but of this much we can be certain—in all of it Christ will be present to him, calling him to the only form of fulfillment that matters—fulfillment in all faith, hope, and love. We can know, with absolute certainty, that (baptized child's name) has been claimed by Christ, and Christ will enrich his life.

On this baptismal Sunday morning, we should be mindful of the world in which we live: a world that is wounded and in which the lonely and forgotten victims of human cruelty often find refuge in some back alley, or on a card-board-bed, feasting from a local dumpster; a world in which might is measured by military prowess, and the poor are still pushed to the margins by an increasingly slim minority of wealthy; a world in which far too many children continue to be victimized in every way. This is not a world different from that in which our Lord Christ turned water into wine; perhaps the only real difference between the world *then* and *now* is a question of the numbers of humans populating the face of the earth. But the world, in its essentials, is basically the same.

I read this to mean that the significance of the sign Christ performed at that wedding in Cana of Galilee has lost none of its power or relevance for our lives, or for the lives of our children and our children's children—the world in which we live, and move, and have our being. And so, this morning, we celebrate the joy our Savior shared with His own disciples, as we again hear this marvelous account of water to wine at Cana in Galilee, blessing us with an image of God's own coming kingdom. And we are blessed with this sacrament of infant baptism, in which we hear once again the same Lord's promise to be with us, for us, and yes, for our children's children, and for the whole of the world as well. We come to this fount, and begin as God's grace would have it, with a word of promise, hope, and decisive certainty that all things will one day find fulfillment in Christ and in the coming kingdom of God. And as we come, we recall the promise of our God spoken through the voice of His prophet Isaiah:

On that Day "the LORD of Hosts will prepare a feast for all the peoples . . . a feast of well-aged wine, choice meat, finely aged wine. . . He will destroy the burial shroud, the shroud over all peoples. He will destroy death forever; (And) the LORD God will wipe away the tears from every face. . . ." Amen.

Nine

John 15:4

Fruit of the Vine

(Jesus said) "Remain in me, and I in you. Just as a branch is unable to produce fruit by itself unless it remains on the vine, so neither can you unless you remain in Me."

ONE OF MY MORE precocious female colleagues asked if I was certain of the wisdom of using "fruit" in my sermon title. She suggested that when it comes to women, the word "fruit" cuts one of two ways. And she has a point. The capacity for some women to become pregnant is, by their own testimony almost effortless; while others, sadly, find pregnancy the one joy in life they'll apparently never experience. In pastoral care I've shared the joy of a couple who announce their first pregnancy, and the anguish of a couple for whom all efforts have failed to bring them that same joy. In other areas of life as well, the word "fruit" can, on the one hand, mean the radiance of joy in abundance, and on the other hand, mean the shadow of a sad or cheerless insufficiency.

For one who is on the favorable side of a "fruitful" experience, whatever the gains, life becomes that much more pleasurable and full; for one on the deficient side of the "fruitful" event, whatever the degree of loss, life can be, and often is, diminished, and hope negligible.

And the fact of life, that some are on the favorable side—with the gains to life apparently unending—while others seem to be trapped on the discouraging side—with the losses in life similarly without end—raises all kinds of questions about the justice of it all. It would only seem reasonable where someone to ask: Where is the justice in the reality that one woman can have as many children as she apparently would desire, while another cannot share in that same joy, even with the vast investment made—financially, emotionally, physically, even spiritually?

Or: Where is the justice in the reality that some, in financial matters, always seem to be on the profitable side of the fruitfulness, while others cannot even lift their heads above the flood waters of financial misfortune? Or again: Where is the justice in the certainty that while some people experience only the abundant side of good health, others seem deprived of even the morsels that fall from the table of fruitful health and well-being? And since we're all sitting in a church this morning, we might pose another question as well: Where is the justice when one church rejoices in abundance of members, while another has known only the deficit side of fruitful membership growth?

I once heard two crop farmers discussing the disparity in the fruitfulness of their individual fields, in the same year, under the same conditions, and with the very same level of care in preparation and fertilization of the soil. Both farms and fields were under the same weather conditions as well. Still, the one said he was sure to have a bumper crop, like none he'd ever seen before, while the other said he was sure this would be the worse harvest he'd seen in some 30 years of farming.

When all is said and done, it would appear that the word and reality of what is often said to be fruitful, does in fact cut one of two ways: either in your favor and with plenty, or to your detriment and with a similar loss. I think it was Erma Bombeck who said, with tongue-in-cheek: "*The same generous sun that warms my neighbor's garden only wilts my houseplants!"* So it seems my colleague was correct; the word *fruitful* often cuts one of two ways, the one exception being with God. The force of the metaphor Jesus uses in this morning's gospel lesson—the image of the grape*vine*—is found in the fact that, with God, there is always a plentitude of what can only be described as fruitfulness, whether of a spiritual, emotional, or even a material kind; with God, the fruit is of one kind only, and that is always in abundance.

Now I'm only too conscious of the fact that for many of us, the concept of God extending in abundance grace, goodness, mercy, joy, fulfillment, and a multitude of other pleasantries in life, does not, on balance, correspond with most of our life experience. In fact, for many of us, there often seems to be a deficit of delight in the fruitful facets of life—even when we have turned to God, seeking God's attention and affections. But we shouldn't measure the truthfulness of what the Bible professes based solely on our experiences in life—whether negative or positive in nature. When Jesus employed the image of the vine in reference to himself, and the necessity that disciples remain attached to him, in order to produce the fruits-of-faith in the power of God's Holy Spirit, he was employing a metaphor—not unlike that of shepherd. Those who first heard Jesus use this metaphor had a large pool of biblical references that also spoke of God as fruitful.

Even if you have limited knowledge of the story of God as found throughout the whole of the Bible, simply consider this: God gave Adam and Eve a garden and all in abundance; God called Abraham and led him to an abundant new life; God freed the Hebrew slaves and fed them in the wilderness with an abundance, while providing water for their parched throats and in abundance; and throughout their long history, God bathed the children of Israel with an abundance of mercy, forgiveness, steadfast love. And Jesus, in John's gospel, said, "I have come that they may have life and have it in abundance." Yet throughout the very same story of God and his people it is patently evident that whenever they chose to drift from his will, to wander from the fold, to disconnect from a vital relationship with the living God — their souls began to wilt and their faith to wither, like a branch broken-off at the stem of a vine.

In the book of the prophet Isaiah it's written of God's people that they were to God like a desirable vineyard and God said, "I, Yahweh, watch over it; I water it regularly. I guard it night and day so that no one disturbs it." And in the book of the prophet Jeremiah, God says to Israel, "I planted you, a choice vine from the very best seed. How then could you turn into a degenerate, foreign vine?" The capacity to know the fruitfulness of faith is dependent upon constancy in the relationship with the God who is the author of all good things in life, and life itself. Jesus said, "Remain in Me, and I in you. Just as the branch is unable to produce fruit by itself unless it remains on the vine, so neither can you unless you remain in Me."

The fruit we are to produce has already been described by Jesus in John's gospel as the love we are to have for one another and others. Such love is the fruit the world will see as testimony to our having remained in Christ. But such love is dependent upon the constancy of our relationship with and in Christ; someone has referred to this as a relationship of loving mutuality. I find this passage immensely comforting in that the word of Jesus intends to encourage us to remain with him—abide in him and stay close to his heart—by remaining faithful to his will. In this marvelous metaphor our Lord has promised us that we can know the fruitful love of God, and just as important, we can bear that same fruit to a world withering on the vine of life for want of such love.

Nothing could be clearer to me from this passage than that we who are branches on the vine of Christ are to focus in faith, not so much on how we can gain from the fruitful love of a gracious Lord, but on how we can give of that same fruit without reserve and feed those who long to be loved on the sweetness of grace we've been given, and in abundance. The grapevine, if fruitful, will hold such an abundance of love that countless souls in crisis will be fed on its richness. I've no doubt, the late Mother Teresa was correct when she said, "The hunger for love is much more difficult to remove than the hunger for bread." And as branches connected to the vine which is Christ, we can offer those who long to be loved, forgiven, and accepted, the fruit of faith.

In abiding, in remaining close to Christ, the fruit of love will be always available to any and all who hunger for those things the world just cannot give. Recall those crop farmers I mentioned earlier in this sermon, the one with a plentiful harvest and the other in deficit? They were members of the church I was serving at the time, and the one who gained the bumper crop shared of his fruitful yield with his neighbor and brother in Christ. They both were blessed.

Spurgeon once said of this passage in which Jesus uses the metaphor of the vine and the fruitful produce of love it implies: "Go measure the heavens with a rule; weigh the mountains in a scale; take the ocean's water and calculate each drop; count the sand upon the sea's wide shore; and when you have accomplished all of this, then you can tell how much (God) loves you!"

The fruitful love of God has been showered upon us and feeds our souls on the vine which is Christ, the vine which is so fruitful it can promote our growth for all of this life and into eternal life. Amen.

Ten

Matthew 19:13
The Touch of Christ

Then children were brought to (Christ) so that He might put His hands on them and pray. But His disciples rebuked them.

THESE WORDS INTRODUCE ONE of the more familiar stories in the gospels, and one of the best-known-and-loved sayings of Jesus: "Leave the children alone, and don't try to keep them from coming to Me, because the kingdom of heaven is made up of people like this." In reading this story and preparing this sermon, I was conscious of how this simple, yet poignant story would have a rather strange twist were it told in today's setting, where "touching" children of any age has become deeply problematic. I imagine that even Christ would be required to sign some form of waver, or to attend a workshop on the improprieties of "touching" children.

I'm not suggesting that such practices are in any way inappropriate or even unnecessary; we are all each of us only too aware of how endangered children of all ages are in this current climate of parental and/or professional misconduct, violated trust, and

Matthew 19:13

horrors of physical, emotional, and sexual abuse. There can be no doubt that we must be protective of our children, as the most vulnerable in any society, even if that should mean policies that some consider excessive in their restrictions. But there's also and at the same time a kind of visceral reaction—a "gut-feeling" if you will—that in our desire, or real need, to protect our children from harm, we inadvertently deny them one of the most vital of human languages—the language of "touch." It's the way of sin to create an environment of mistrust, with threatened abuse of something that can be a treasured expression of intimacy—human touch.

Perhaps you too read the recent study that explored the importance of human touch for hospice clients and hospital patients in the final stages of life. The study concluded that those deprived of human touch display a far greater degree of anxiety and restlessness in those closing moments of life, than do those who are bathed in human touch. The researchers stated that for all 400 cases, with one exception, testimony of the dying was unanimously that they felt *untouchable*, as though death itself were a contagious disease. Those interviewed stated that they thrived on the human care and kindness of others conveyed and received by the simplest touch of a human hand.

In the historical period of Christ's earthly ministry it was the children who were considered *untouchable*—regardless of age—children were often deprived of this basic human expression of love and parental care. Apparently, if we are to take the testimony of the gospel writers seriously, Jesus dismantled this social taboo, making it a regular practice to both touch the children and to invite them into the inner circle of his disciples. Mark's account is by the far the most graphic, closing this story by saying that "After taking them in His arms, (Jesus) laid His hands on them and blessed them."

And should you be curious as to what exactly was conferred when Jesus "laid His hands on them and blessed them," simply recall the story of Isaac and his sons Esau and Jacob. To lay-on hands, so as to confer a blessing, was to grant the one being blessed all of the benefits, privileges of inheritance; in this singular act with children, Christ was conferring on each, all the riches of grace and glory that would come to those chosen to become members of His Father's kingdom.

Interesting, isn't it? Christ does not suggest that the children learn from the adults what it means to be mature in terms of spiritual realities and as prerequisite for discipleship. That, too, runs counter to what we'd expect to be the case; we're the ones who "mentor" the children in the best ways of following Christ, in what qualifies as faithfulness. I assure you those immediate to Jesus thought the same, which is why His comment is so counter-cultural.

Christ states in a dramatic manner that it isn't the children who need to be our students and should become like adults, but adults should take-on the very best characteristics of a child. Notice I said the very best characteristics; even a child can demonstrate the effects of sin in his or her attitude and actions. Christ points to those characteristics that set children apart. Things like: vulnerability; dependence on others for welfare and well-being; a curiosity about almost everything, and almost every aspect of life, yet to be explored; limited defenses against the expression of the most common human emotion; imaginative and creative energies; the ability to dream of worlds like this one and yet with far more enchantment. There are other characteristics as well, many you've most likely thought of even as I shared my limited list.

You see, as I've come to understand this life—it's not only that we grow-up and grow-old—it's also true that we grow-*out*-of-some-incredibly-wonderful-ways of looking at, appreciating, and being in our world. Too often, far too many of us grow-out of those child-like characteristics like the capacity to imagine, to dream, to see the world as a wonder, or to remain exposed to what other adults think exaggeration. I doubt that it was any different in the time of Christ's earthly ministry; after all, we adults have our responsibilities, don't we? That's always been true; so the disciples of Jesus try to prevent these bothersome children from distracting their Master as He sets about the significant work of teaching them. This discipleship and kingdom of God stuff is quite serious

Matthew 19:13

business—a very weighty undertaking—not to be entrusted to children as we all know children are prone to make light of matters of grave importance to adults.

Have you noticed? Jesus has this tendency to turn things upside-down-inside-out, and in doing so, leaves us questioning what in the world we're to make of such incongruous teachings. Are we to take His lesson *literally* and not merely *seriously*? Well, the clue for us is found in two words employed by Mark in portrayal of this same occasion: *welcome* and *like*. Jesus said, "I assure you: Whoever does not *welcome* the kingdom of God *like* a child will never enter it."

Whenever I visit my grandchildren, I'm greeted as though they hadn't seen me for years. Maybe you know what I mean; they greet me with excitement, joy, and even anticipation, and it doesn't seem to matter that I'd just visited with them the week before. I believe that's what Jesus means when He speaks of "welcoming" the kingdom of God "like" a child—having a heart that greets the Gospel and the presence of the Holy Spirit with joy, and excitement, and even anticipation of mysterious happenings that come with the Spirit's presence.

Over time even those with a deep commitment to being the best disciple, grow-out-of the joy, fascination, and excitement that come with the first blush of the new convert to Christianity.

That is why those of us who have been disciples for a long time need this teaching of Jesus as much, if not more, than those who are new to the faith. We need to return to a place of spiritual dependency and trust in the goodness of Him who is called "our Father." We need to ask the Lord to place within our hearts that sense of child-like joy and fascination with the things of faith. We need to allow the Holy Spirit to create in our hearts that hope which, like a child anticipating the miracle of Christmas morning, will cause us to relish a future we've yet to experience but believe, in faith, will one Day be our reality. We need to recapture that sense of curiosity that will drive us, each day, to seek a deeper and ever greater degree of divine wisdom.

We need to reaffirm that we are children of a God whose love is unending.

But most of all we need, each day, to submit to the mentoring of the Spirit of Christ, who alone can lead us to a faith, hope, and love that, even though growing into mature adults, we will never out-grow-the-need-for-God's-grace. Amen.

Eleven

John 21:4–5
Morning Came

Morning came, and there stood Jesus on the beach, but his disciples did not know that it was Jesus. He called out to them, "Friends, have you caught anything?" They answered, "No." He said, "Cast the net to the right side of the boat, and you'll catch some!" (New English Bible)

OUR GOSPEL TEXT FOR this morning has the same narrative begin *at dawn*, while other translations have the same passage read, *at the break of a new dawn*, or, *when daybreak came*, or, *early the next day*. The translation I've chosen, *Morning came*, is one of the best for both its simplicity and accuracy as an English equivalent to the original Greek. Yet all translations convey the power and significance of the phrase John has chosen to open this story of a resurrection appearance.

As you already know—if you're familiar with the four Gospels—John's is the only Gospel to recount this particular event. The way in which he's chosen to open the story is intentionally a mirror reflection of the language all four Gospels use in their

Easter morning narratives, which is—*early Sunday morning*—or a phrasing close to the same.

In using a similar wording John connects these two resurrection appearances, as if he were intent on having the reader or hearer associate one appearance with the other; in other words, both appearances are making a similar claim, theologically: The risen Christ encounters His followers at the break of a *new day*, with a *new* command, *new* ministry, and *new* hope held-out to their aching hearts. Although only two words—*morning came*—the phrase conveys a colossal truth for each us and all of us.

We all, each of us, have experienced or will experience occasions when the night is long, dark, and wearisome—as sleep seems to escape us, staring at the ceiling grows old, and nothing holds our attention for long, with the exception of whatever it is haunting our mind and heart.

And there are similar experiences: the spouse who waits all night for the surgeon to bring word; the parent, kneeling at the bed-side of her ailing child; the patient recently diagnosed with cancer. Of course, it only stands to reason, that the night is a time for rest and rejuvenation—and much of the time, for most of us, that's realized, isn't it? But we also know ourselves, or have known another, for whom there are nights long in waiting and short on sleep. And then morning comes—it always comes—and there's another day.

Yet each new day holds for us as much *mystery* as it does *promise*; no one of us has that crystal ball with the capacity to see clearly what will be faced on any given day, as dawn breaks. We have no way of knowing, with absolute certainty, the issue or issues we'll face on any given day, and bring them with us—at the end of the day—a huge weight of apprehension and anxiety on our chest—as we lay our head on the pillow. Even so—there remains a certain effect of dawn, the night giving way to light, the appearance of the sun on the horizon—that can and often will awaken in us a sense of anticipation and hope—even if only like the flickering flame of a candle, there's hope.

John 21:4–5

And I assure you, it was no different for those who wrote, read, or heard the Gospel for the first time; they too knew long nights of apprehension and sleeplessness—and a faint hope with each new day. The account that precedes the appearance of Jesus on the beach, follows the very first appearance, first to the eleven in the absence of the one disciple—Thomas—and then the second appearance to all eleven.

Here's what I find almost inconceivable; even after *two appearances* of the risen Christ with them and for them—the *only* option they saw open to them was to return to the all-too familiar trade of fishing. It was sometime following the appearances and, as John tells us, Peter said, "I am going out fishing." To which the others said, "We'll go with you."

I find it remarkable that, to a disciple, they all chose to go fishing! Not that I have a problem with "fishing," of course; but because prior to the call to follow Christ, they were not all of them fisherman. Just read any account of their call to follow and you'll see. But on this occasion—even after Christ had been revealed as the resurrected Lord of life and death, they *all* chose to take-up the trade of fishing. The only reasonable explanation to be made is that John had a very significant theological claim to make in recording this staggering event; and that is to demonstrate the fulfillment of Christ's call, when He said: "Follow Me, and I will make you become fishers of men!"

This fishing expedition is symbolic of the larger form of fishing to which each of them and all of them had been called by Christ. What makes this scene significant is the result of their effort. John tells us: "But that night they caught nothing." Small wonder! John has dramatized the truth of Christ's claim, who, while still with them—in the flesh—had advised them saying: "Apart from Me you can do nothing!" They'd now lived the truth! All of this is prelude to the very first thing Christ has them do when He appears to them from the beach; He commands them to try *again*—and directs them to "the catch," which is so large, John tells us, they could not haul the net aboard, there were so many fish in it. And, as the saying goes: There it is! "Apart from *Me* you can do *nothing*," spectacularly realized.

And let's not miss one of the *crucial* points: All of this transpired only when *morning* had come, on a *new* day, with the *dawn* of another day, and *only* in the Presence of Christ—the resurrected Lord of life and ministry. It's the Presence and under the empowerment of Christ our Risen/Reigning Lord that any and all ministry generates significant fruit, or as in the analogy with fishing—a huge haul! In short: *without* the Savior and His empowerment, ministry is all but useless. Like those disciples out there on that lake, having caught nothing after a night of—what must have been—exhausting labor, we need to be attentive and obedient to the direction of our Lord in the power of His Holy Spirit. Ministry is—and all forms of ministry are—made possible only in and by the Presence and Power of Christ.

But that isn't all we're given in this gospel lesson; we're also assured that regardless of the kind of night we must sometimes endure—a night of sleepless anxiety, a night of worried awaiting, a night filled with dismay, a night of loneliness, a night of dejection or despair—when

Morning comes Christ will shine the miracle of His grace into our hearts and enlighten us with a living hope. Even if only a flicker, it will be sufficient for the person of faith, who entrusts all to the Risen/Reigning Savior.

I find it compelling to note that the *birth* of Christ was heralded by a star and the *resurrection* of Christ was declared by the sun's rising on a new day; one, *the star*, high above the world below, and the other, *the sun*, in close proximity of the earth—the world. Heaven and earth are brought together in and around the coming of the Christ into this world. Perhaps this too is symbolic of our need to keep both in clear and intentional relation: heaven and earth, spirituality and service, life and eternal life, the things of God and things of human existence.

Phillips Brooks put it this way: "The glory of the star, the glory of the sun—we must not lose either to the other. We must not be so full of the hope of heaven that we cannot do our work on earth; we must not be so lost in the work of the earth that we shall not be inspired by the hope of heaven."

In light of our morning lesson from John's gospel perhaps we should add that we mustn't be so lost in the darkness of night, we fail to rejoice in the glory of the light that is certain to come at the dawn of a new day. Because, you see my brothers and sisters, the presence of Christ at dawn only assures us that He has been there throughout that long and dark night as well. He promised: "I will never leave you or forsake you." No surprise here; but I'd say that the lessons to be gleaned from John's Gospel are well-worth learning. For, as surely as day follows night, so Christ follows His children throughout the whole of life and makes His Presence the point of our greatest and most resilient hope. Amen.

Twelve

John 13:34-35
Our Heritage

(Christ said): "I give you a new commandment: Love one another. Just as I have loved you, you must also love one another. By this all people will know that you are My disciples, if you have love for one another."

WHEN I WAS A child my maternal grandmother, who came to this country from Ireland when she was only six-teen years of age, would have me and my siblings sit as she told us stories of her home and childhood in Ireland. She would always close her accounts by saying, "You are blessed because you have the rich history of both Ireland and America as your heritage." Of course it was only years later that I came to understand exactly what she meant; a *heritage* is very different from an *inheritance*—with dissimilar obligations.

I came to see the heritage of which my grandmother spoke as both the ground and the substance of my self-understanding—a rich and diverse heritage that informed my own personal history, as well as becoming my responsibility to cherish and *pass-on* to my child and grandchildren. Where an inheritance can be and often

John 13:34-35

is something material to be used, often abused, or even used-up; a heritage is immaterial, some might even say—"spiritual"—and shapes the person of that legacy in ways that are far more profound than could any inheritance. Said in the simplest of terms: An inheritance is something we possess, while a heritage is that which—if you will—possesses us! Losing a sense of *heritage* is a far greater loss and is much more damaging to one's sense of self-identity than would be the depletion or total loss of any singular form of material or physical *inheritance*. Our identity as individuals, as families, as community, as church, and as Christian disciples, has a foundation in a particular heritage.

When the Lord Jesus told His disciples, "I give you a new command: Love one another," He was doing more than provide them with a moral or ethical floor plan for the way forward and in faith; Christ was conferring upon them—and all who would come after them—a given *heritage*. He was stating that all who would come to embrace Him as Savior and Lord would also take-up a heritage with origins in the very heart of God; a heritage to be shared—passed-on—to others. Christ's "new command" wasn't merely something to be *done*—as if some outward practice, or exercise of the human will; Christ was bestowing upon those immediate to His voice—and all who would take-up the easy yoke of ministry in His name—a new sense of self-identity or as the apostle Paul stated it: "a new creation." Of course, like any other heritage we receive, it's in our own free-will to either pass-it-on faithfully to the next generation—or hold it so close to our breast that we end-up treating it more as an inheritance—for us, and our benefit alone—than we do as the heritage Christ intended it to be—shared in all liberality, generously.

And the reason it's so absurd for any individual disciple or group of followers to treat this love, this heritage, as a benefit to them alone, is the fact that, this particular love Christ confers as heritage, simply evaporates when treated as nothing more than an inheritance. There's no more expedient way to assure the loss of this precious love Christ has bestowed than to withhold it from another or others—regardless of our reasons for doing so; it's a contradiction in terms to speak of a Christian who must work at loving others; there are no stingy saints.

Even more urgently, as this world increasingly becomes a wasteland in which there is a deficiency of such—"love divine, all loves excelling"—it has become more crucial that we, who have received this blessed heritage from our Lord, pass-it-on-to-others with liberality and great generosity—in caring, compassion, and selfless acceptance of those who've been estranged from Christ and His Church—for all the wrong reasons.

If there's any one single factor that causes others to view the Church of Christ with a skeptical eye—it's the apparent deficiency of a generous acceptance as the hallmark of Christ-like love, the very heritage that should be at the heart and soul of any Christian and any congregation; and not simply because we are commanded to love in this way, but because Christ graciously *confers* this love upon us *as Church*. I swear to you—I'm not making this up for the sake of dramatic presentation of the point—Christ said: "By this all people will know that you are My disciples, if you have love for one another." "Love for one another," means love that is so evident it will immediately impact anyone entering the community of faith in worship, in fellowship, in ministry. This heritage of Christ-like love is to become the single-most-important mark of spiritual identity; the Church of Christ is evident not by the beauty of its houses of worship, or by its number of worshippers, or by its success in raising funds for its mission and ministry.

The Church of Christ is evident wherever this heritage of love is manifest—without regard to any one characteristic of the recipient, and without reservation. The Church of Christ is seen whenever and wherever this love prevails.

Picture—if you will—a turtle without a shell, or a peacock without plumage, or horse without legs—each would be far less than it was created to be by our God. Christ has created the Church in love—to share love and to spread love—the love of God which, as was affirmed by the apostle Paul "passes all understanding." That simply means that God's love—in particular when such love is poured-out, passed-on, to human hearts—is as deep a mystery

John 13:34–35

as it is distinct in reality. The great D.L. Moody once said that "Joy is love exalted; peace is love in repose; long-suffering is love enduring; gentleness is love in society; compassion is love in action; faith is love on the battlefield of life; humility is love in the act of forgiveness; patience is love in training."

There's no other place in the world, save the Church and in the heart and soul of each individual disciple, where the claim can be made to have received the precious heritage of our Savior's love—not for save-keeping, but for abundant—and—confident—sharing. We spread this heritage of love, as freely as does the sower with his seed, and do so with the full assurance of the word of our God, that when such love falls on the fertile soils of a human soul—it will produce—and produce abundantly!

Someone has said that, "if love is the soul of Christian existence, it must be at the heart of every other Christian virtue.... No virtue is truly a virtue unless it is permeated, or informed, by love." And I couldn't agree more! Christ-like-love is as much the heritage of any Christian heart as is his or her familial lineage, ethnicity, or place of origin. We are re-created to love!

Most of us are aware of the fact that the apostle Paul devoted an entire chapter in his first letter to the church in the ancient city of Corinth, paying tribute to that form of love which is our heritage; we are only too familiar with the poetry of Paul's accolade, when he writes "Love bears all things, believes all things, hopes all things, endures all things. Love never ends."

And I've yet to discover a more helpful interpretation of exactly what Paul was saying than that provided by the pen of Karl Barth. Barth said, to understand the whole of first Corinthians, chapter thirteen, one need only exchange the title of "Christ" for the word "love." When we do, we get this: Christ bears all things, believes all things, hopes all things, endures all things. Christ never ends. The heritage received from Christ is not merely His love, but Him!

When we live our lives in the love He has given us, we pass-on to a weary and wounded world, the very Presence of Christ to those in pain, those perplexed by life, those lost and lonely souls

The Gospel of Grace for Wounded Sojourners

who seem to have forgotten that they're loved beyond measure by the Master we serve, the Savior who's never—even for a moment—lost sight of His suffering children. Most of us will never do great things; but with the heritage we've received in Christ, we can do even the smallest measure of ministry and mission, with the greatest love the world has ever known. Amen.

Thirteen

Mark 1:38–39

He Came Preaching

And (Jesus) said to (His disciples): "Let's go on to the neighboring villages so that I may preach there too. This is why I have come." So He went into all Galilee, preaching in their synagogues and driving our demons.

THESE WORDS OF CHRIST, as recorded in Mark's gospel, constitute one of several claims Jesus made for both Himself and His purpose for coming into the world. What's most striking about Christ's claim, "Let's go on to the neighboring villages so that I may preach . . . This is why I have come," is the power implicit in this remarkably straight-forward statement of His purpose; in other words, the assertion that He'd come into the world to proclaim a message—that is to say—to preach. And here's the reason I find this claim so extraordinary. Seldom do we think of the message, proclamation, or preaching of Christ as equivalent in power and significance to the miracles of healing, or to raising the dead, or even to His own resurrection.

And yet, it would appear that—according to His own personal assertion—it's precisely His preaching that should be the central focus of faith. Of course, Christ could just as easily have claimed that He came into the world to astound it with God's power to bring about healing and restoration of the dead, or to demonstrate authority over the forces of nature. Yet, that is not His affirmation of the most essential reason for—what we've come to call—the incarnation. The implications for you and for me, and in our own discipleship, are equally momentous, and we'll explore that in a moment. But first, we have to explore the inference of Christ's claim for His own ministry.

The first thing to be said is that Mark isn't alone in his testimony to the place Jesus Himself gave to His preaching—His *message*. There's perhaps no more familiar passage than that found in the first chapter of John's gospel, in which he affirms the centrality of the message of Christ as being incarnate—enfleshed—in Jesus Himself: "In the beginning was the Word, and the Word was with God, and the Word was God . . . and the Word became flesh and took up residence among us." Matthew and Luke are far more subtle in asserting the connection between the preaching and message of Jesus and His person, but they do proclaim the same; that is to say, that *what* Jesus taught and *who* He was cannot be detached. Mark records Jesus as saying, in essence, I came into the world to preach the Gospel of Grace. And if Christ has so stated the case—that His primary purpose for coming into the world was to "preach"—we would do well to see clearly just how it is that—in His case—the *message* and *Messenger* were and are one and the same!

Let's use an analogy: Let's suppose that you've made a promise to someone, not just your promise to do this or that, but something of far greater consequence. Let's say you've promised that you will always be ready to serve the needs of another, regardless of the time of day or night your services are required. You see how that implies not just a spoken word, but a spoken word that demands you place yourself in that promise whenever you are called to serve the other in fulfillment of that promise? Perhaps that's as close as

Mark 1:38-39

we can get to grasping how Christ's *being*—and His *message*—were and are one-and-the-same.

Yet the implications of this astounding affirmation are where we see the gracious benefit to us. Because, you see, if the person and the message of Christ are one-and-the-same, then whatever it is He is said to have taught—in the gospels as we now have them—is invested with His person as well. When Christ teaches that He is "the Way, the Truth, and the Life"—He's not merely saying that His words, this message alone, must be embraced if we're to find the *Way*, or come to know the *Truth*, or find personal fulfillment in the *Life* that God has promised. Christ is actually asserting that in order for one to find the *Way*, so as to recognize *Truth*, in order to identify the full-richness-of-*Life* as God intended—one must embrace *Him*, because *He* and the *message* of the Gospel are one-and-the-same. Salvation isn't to be found merely in the message—but in the Messenger.

The greatest miracle of all, in the full accounting of the life and ministry of Christ as recorded in all four of our gospels, isn't in those stunning events of healing, raising the dead, or making nature obey His voice and command. The most astounding miracle of all is that Christ came into the world to bear a message from the Lord God—from the very heart of the Father—to each of us and all of us together. Whenever, wherever, and however the Gospel is preached, there is also the real and gracious presence of Christ to be discovered.

The apostle Paul declared the very same when he wrote this to the church in Rome: "For I am not ashamed of the gospel, because it is God's power for salvation to everyone who believes, first to the Jew, and also to the Greek. For in it God's righteousness is revealed from faith to faith, just as it is written: The righteous will live by faith" (Rom. 1:16–17). And in another—the author of the Letter to the Hebrews –asserts that "the word of God is living and effective and sharper than any double-edged sword, penetrating as far as the separation of soul and spirit, joints and marrow" (Heb. 4:12a). Such assertions can only be made by Paul, as for all authors in the New Testament, because the message of God as declared by

Christ and Christ as Messenger are so bound together they cannot, ever, be separated one from the other. Where the word of the Gospel is, Christ is, and where Christ is there is always the promise and the power of salvation.

Now we're better prepared to see how all of this relates to the ministry and mission we share as disciples of this Christ.

One of the more evident implications for our shared ministry is that we needn't be obsessed with activities as the measurement of our faithfulness as a church. All too often churches tend to think that the *more* they are *doing*, the more faithful they are *being* to the call of Christ to serve; in other words, an *active* church is a more faithful church. Yet if one employed the ministry of Christ Himself as exemplary of this model for the church—well, He was a miserable failure! In fact—over and over again—the gospels portray Christ as the One who accomplishes far *more*, by doing far *less*. Whatever Christ does was done after much prayer and patient waiting for the guidance of the Spirit. And just as important, this morning's gospel lesson portrays Christ as having seen His ultimate purpose in proclaiming the Good News.

Perhaps the church, then, needs to be less obsessed with *doing*, with *activity*, and more concerned with how fervently and faithfully she takes-up the mission of preaching, proclaiming, the Good News; and that means telling people the story—as in—"I love to tell the story of unseen things above; of Jesus and His glory, of Jesus and His love." Recall, for a moment now, how Jesus Himself said that He'd come to bring this message, this preaching, this "good news," first to the whole house of Israel—to the People of God—those one would have thought knew the "story" by heart and took it to heart. Obviously, that was not the case, which is why we must also tell that same message again and again within the church herself: "I love to tell the story, for those who know it best, Seem hungering and thirsting to hear it like the rest."

Well—one would hope so! Yet, in our contemporary church, evidence seems to suggest something else altogether; both knowing it *best* and the *hungering and thirsting* are questionable realities—not unlike Israel in the time of Jesus. And that makes this

Mark 1:38-39

ministry of proclamation—even in our own house, so to speak—all the more imperative. To contend that faithful proclamation of the Gospel is more evident in action than in speech cannot be sustained by the testimony to the ministry of Christ Himself, where preaching, proclamation is said to be the vital reason for His ministry and mission.

    I assure you that whether in the fellowship of the church or in the sorry state of this hurting-world, it's this proclamation of "Good News"—the message of forgiveness, mercy, grace, and the open and inviting arms of our Heavenly Father—that is needed as much—if not more—than any one particular action or activity we might undertake. Jesus said, ". . . this is why I have come;" to proclaim; to preach; to spread abroad this glorious gospel of God. Surely, as disciples, as *church*, as *body of Christ*, we can do no less. Amen.

Fourteen

John 18:36

Christ's Kingdom

"My kingdom is not of this world," Jesus said. "If My kingdom were of this world, My servants would fight, so that I wouldn't be handed over to the Jews. As it is, My kingdom does not have its origin here."

PERHAPS YOU ARE, AS I was, unfamiliar with the hymn entitled, *"Eternal Christ, You Rule."* The verses of this hymn are based on the words of Jesus from this morning's sermon text as found in the *Gospel of John*. The first two verses of the hymn read:

> Eternal Christ, You rule—keeping company with pain;
>
> Enduring ridicule, rejection—still—You reign.
>
> Eternal Christ, You rule—speaking pardon from the cross, taking-on sin's deadly cost;
>
> Forgiving pounded nails—death did its worst and lost!

Often we forget how, in Christ Jesus, God has already won the ultimate victory; the victory that matters most as we, or a loved one, come to draw that final breath. This victory over death

John 18:36

and the grave was one that only our God could have won. No one human heart, soul, and spirit could've won this victory over the enemy whose countenance alone is sufficient to conquer human courage. God brought light and life into the realm of human life's most ruinous experience; that is to say, *death*.

And yet, it's easy to forget that same truth, in particular when some life event adds fear to frustration or powerlessness to human pain. In the midst of our most grievous circumstances, we yearn for a word of encouragement and hope beyond all humanly fabricated hope. When faced with some crisis or other, we find that faith and belief in the possibilities of God doing something to reverse the course of our crisis become weakened to the point of being all but ineffectual.

Perhaps we search for some source of actual security, some anchor for our anxious spirit, some certainty that this crisis will not break the back of our faith in God. In the severest of situations we seek to gain a foothold for our faith, a place where we can shelter our soul until the stormy gales have subsided. Stinging situations often provoke questions regarding the meaning of life and our shared future. The magnitude of the experience of crisis has little or no bearing on how deeply run feelings of apprehension and anxiety; whether it's a crisis of terrorism or the rumor that the company is situated for lay-offs makes little difference. We know how it is that critical events lead to limping or lame faith. Such circumstances can create, in even the most devoted Christian, a profound sense of gloom concerning the future and some troubling questions as well.

What's it all about? Where will it all end and what will become of us? Has God hidden Himself away in the tranquility of heaven and given-up on this world and we humans as if a lost cause? Can we have confidence in the incredible promises of God?

There're far too many situations in this world that can cause us to question or perhaps even forget: God has already won for us, and in Christ Jesus, the ultimate victory over death and destruction, over despair and pain-driven disbelief, over that oldest and most formidable of foes, the sinister-spirit whose only goal is our complete destruction and whose only weapon is the lie:

"God does not care; you are alone in this old world; nothing will ever come of this Christian gospel and faith!" Here in this sacred space we must not seek to shelter ourselves from the more graphic ruptures of this world and life; we must not hide in hymns, prayers, or preaching, from the more dreadfulness of the crisis faced in living. It's of no service to our faith or our Lord to come here with the expectation of "getting away from all of that ugly and bitter stuff we see and hear and have to deal with all week long!" In fact, it's here that we come to hear and embrace the only Word with *transformative* power.

There're occasions when, in the activities of the day-to-day living, we are given glimpses of something sacred, spiritually fulfilling, or gratifying– something soothing to our hearts and souls. Whether cleaning the house, strapped down to a desk or lap top, or pouring over papers to grade, there are hints and glimpses of heaven that touch the edges of our experience. Maybe we even catch the scent of a perfumed angel as someone in the lunchroom pauses for prayer over a brown-paper-bag. It could be on the commute home, and we see a billboard we must have passed a thousand and one times before and never took notice that it was the image of a cross, a crown, and the empty tomb. Or we're struck by the gleam of a church's steeple in the golden glow of a setting autumnal sun. There are moments when the daily world is touched by some aspect of transcendence—the grace of God; but what about when we're seated in this sacred-space?

Here we are all and always reminded of the mystery and the majesty of God; God whose very presence we question whenever we face another hardship, personal or global. In this single hour we practice sacred arts, lost on the rest of the world, arts that have a history exceeding two thousand years. Here we speak language and engage in ritual and artistic practices foreign to every other moment of our day-to-day living. In this sacred-space we listen to stories and sayings distant and strange to the contemporary world, where we spend the majority of our time. It's only in this space that

John 18:36

we take bread and cup and speak of a communion with Him who is the creator of all; it's only in this space that parents bring their child to a fount filled with water, believing that in this simplest act, their infant is claimed by Christ for membership in His Church.

Consider for a moment the mystery wrapped-up in just one responsive prayer of the liturgy: "Lord, have mercy; Christ, have mercy; Lord, have mercy." Where else in the world would we dare use such elevated, *extra*-ordinary language as this? One hour each week we gather to worship; and the language we use reminds the world—*God is*! He can be pushed to the parameters of culture and society—but God will not simply fade away in silence. This is His world, and He has sacrificed far too much to simply abandon it.

It's this God of Abraham, Isaac, and Jacob—this God and Father of our Lord Jesus Christ—who has won for us and for the world the ultimate victory over all that is now vicious, vindictive, vengeful, and violent to the core. This God has conquered each and every form of calamity or crisis that would threaten to rob us of life's pleasure and purpose. So that every Sunday, as the Lord's Day, represents a time for us to lift-up our heads—lift them high above the humdrum and dreariness of the daily routines—allowing for our souls and spirits to be lifted above the pain of a life often plagued by the less-than-pleasurable.

What do you think? Can we lift our eyes beyond all that is chaotic and catastrophic in this world, or even in our own personal sphere of existence, and behold something sacred, spectacular, of a far greater glory than we might otherwise believe possible? Can we claim the language of John's Jesus as truth, not just *our* truth, truth for the *whole of the world*, when He responded to Pilate, saying: "My kingdom is not of this world . . . My kingdom does not have its origin here." Because, you see, Jesus is telling us that His supreme rule and His unquestioned sovereignty—that's what He means by use of "kingdom"—cannot be defeated, and will not be overtaken by any dark, destructive forces. Once it had been established in His first advent into this world, there was no going back—only forward—ever forward; an unrelenting march forward into the coming kingdom of God, as the fulfillment of the present rule of Christ.

His authority to rule this world, now and into the future, has been given Him by God, His Father; it is an authority that is—as I've said so often—*imperious*! Christ allows no other sovereignty to lay final claim to the lives of His children—His Church—or to exert some ultimate power over their future. Christ *alone* has determined our future, our destiny, our end—which is a beginning of eternal life in His Father's kingdom of fulfillment.

If we can claim the word and vision of Jesus as our truth, we can live in the light of a victory God has won; a victory which will one Day be completed in the coming of His Kingdom.

And in claiming that truth we'll find the courage of faith which is the power to comfort the dying, to reach-out in compassion to the sorrowing, to shoulder the burdens of the sick and the suffering; to say to a world in which the wounded are too often ignored: "Behold, today is the day of salvation, of healing, and of hope!"

There are moments when we live with defeat tasting like ashes in our mouths. Congregations die, slowly, because they stubbornly refuse to remain in the will of the Lord; marriages twist in on themselves with hatred, anger, and an unforgiving spirit. Sometimes we feel unappreciated by those in whom we have invested so much emotion; sometimes we feel as though we're trapped in a terrible job, working for a harsh task-master; sometimes we live with broken bodies or broken spirits or battered souls. And then life looks pointless!

At such times we need the strong note of victory which resounds in the affirmation of Jesus: "My kingdom is not of this world . . . My kingdom does not have its origins here." It's just here we're told that there's a truth far greater than even our greatest fear, a truth that is God's and is a promise with power to bring redemption and healing and hope. A truth that can serve as our finest security: Christ is Sovereign! Christ Reigns! Christ will rule this world until He hands-over His kingly authority to the Father in the coming kingdom of God:

John 18:36

Eternal Christ, You rule—keeping company with pain;
Enduring ridicule, rejected, and still You reign.

Eternal Christ, You rule—speaking pardon from the cross—taking-on sin's deadly cost;

Forgiving pounded nails; death did its worst, and lost!
Amen.

Fifteen

Luke 21:25–28
Faint from Fear

(Jesus said) "There will be signs in the sun, moon, and stars; and there will be anguish on the earth among nations bewildered by the roaring sea and waves. People will faint from fear and expectation of the things that are coming on the world, because the celestial powers will be shaken. Then they will see the Son of Man coming in a cloud with great power and glory. But when these things begin to take place, stand up and lift up your heads, because your redemption is near!"

THIS SEEMS A SOMEWHAT daunting way to begin this holy season of Advent; with all of this dire prediction of a cataclysmic end to the world as spoken by Jesus. After all, we tend not to associate Advent with all of that dark and foreboding imagery; rather, Advent is for most of us anticipatory. But what we anticipate is a far cry from this strikingly ominous image Jesus has painted for us in this word. For most of us this season of Advent is a time to make preparations for the joyous celebration of Christmas—with all of those wonderful images we tend to associate with this singu-

Luke 21:25-28

lar holiday: the gathering together of family and friends for good food and fellowship.

It's safe to say that if we'd been the one to select a Gospel text for this first Sunday of Advent in the year 2012, I doubt very much that we'd have chosen this passage, with its disturbing reference to some graphically grotesque end-time event when "people will faint from fear and expectation of the things that are coming on the world, because the celestial powers will be shaken." That's anything but the kind of language we connect with bright lights, gaily wrapped packages, tinsel, caroling, and ginger-bread men. So, the question becomes: What are we to do with this teaching of Jesus? Are we to simply ignore it, as some form of primitive language, representing a worldview so far removed from our own, we can't relate to it?

Maybe we should've looked more closely at one of the other two lessons of the lection—passing over this Gospel lesson as obsolete—of little or no significance for us. Obviously, I don't think either of these suggestions acceptable, and obviously I'm about to tell you why. I'll begin by helping us gain some clarity on this kind of biblical language and imagery—which were both quite common in the time of Christ, and long before His first advent into this world. Because this language, and the imagery it conveys, cannot be ignored, anymore than we could ignore the Sermon on the Mount, or the Parables of Jesus. The language is called *eschatology* and the imagery is called *apocalyptic*; the term *eschatology* refers to language about the end-of-time, or better said, the *fulfillment* of time and all that God intends for creature and creation, while the term *apocalyptic* is best translated as the "revelation" or "disclosure" of something formally hidden from human view, understanding, or knowledge.

Both were so much a part of Christ's worldview, that to eliminate them from His teaching would be tantamount to stripping Jesus of a central and vital aspect of His message to His world and our own. In other words, the Gospel is nothing if it is not seen to be both *apocalyptic* and *eschatological*, or said again and differently: The Gospel is as much about the *future*, as it is about *past* and *present*. Avoiding those theological and technical terms, I'll state it this way: The Gospel of Christ is a word that speaks to our redemption from *past* sins and dire consequences, our *present* growth and maturation in grace and in Christ, and our own *future fulfillment* in the coming kingdom of God. And, as I've said so often, not our fulfillment only, but the fulfillment of all things in the complete restoration God intends for the whole of His creation—that is to say, the entire cosmos.

I suppose a question would be: Why did Jesus Christ deem it both necessary and essential to use strikingly dreadful terms in reference to the future? In other words, was Jesus predicting a particular and frightening end to the world, or was His use of this language and the associated images for some other purpose? And what might the significance be for our Advent observance?

The question as to "why" Jesus used such language and imagery is, perhaps, the easier of the two to answer: Christ used this particular language and associated imagery to emphasize the escalation of evil, and its effects in the course of human history, and—dramatically—as the time approaches for the advent of God's kingdom as the end to all things evil, deplorable and destructive. There's a sense in which the presence of all we think of as representative of evil will intensify as the kingdom of God draws ever closer; evil will begin to feel the pinch of urgency!

That isn't to say that one can "predict" exactly *when* the "end" will come, simply by measuring the level of escalation in evil events. It's, rather, an affirmation that "evil" is motivated to bring about destruction of all God holds dear; in other words, evil is determined. It's just because "evil" has such determination that it will intensify as it sees the advance of God's coming kingdom. This teaching of Christ also indicates that evil should never be treated as some abstract, impersonal force.

Throughout the Bible evil is personified—spoken of in personal terms—because it mimics all of those same traits and characteristics we connect with a personal being—even though it's really a parasite and must feed-off the existence of genuinely living beings—namely—us. That's simply another way of indicating the

Luke 21:25–28

need for us to take *seriously* evil's intent to twist and turn all that is good and godly into something distasteful and destructive of God's desire for creature and creation. God's coming victory—in Christ and in His Church—is the fuel generating the escalation of evil's efforts to counter with ruinous intent. All of which is why we need to hear in this teaching the promise of Christ as well as His word of warning. He said: "But when these things begin to take place, stand up and lift up your heads, because your redemption is drawing near!"

The intensification of suffering brought on by the intentions of evil is everywhere and always out-matched by the ever greater promise of redemption; that is, the restoration of all beauty, all goodness, all peace, all joy in the coming of Christ—*past, present, and future*. We can endure the effects of evil, today and again tomorrow, only because the presence and promise of Christ, to be with us and to redeem us from all things twisted and ugly, is our sacred strength.

Evil can and will intensify its effects—but it will never prevent God's promise from attaining fulfillment.

Advent is the season in which Christians re-enact, as remembrance, the eagerness for Christ's first "advent"—His first coming—into our world—for us and for our salvation. It's the season in which we also anticipate, in hope and with joy, the promise that He will one Day return—as His second "advent" into our world, to complete the ministry of redemption, in the establishment of a new creation—minus all that is sinful, ugly, and evil. Between the historical framework of Christ's "first" and "second" advents, evil will continue to use every force within its means to frustrate and disrupt God's work of redemption in this world. Yet we who believe in Christ must stand straight, in the face of each and every form of evil, knowing as we do that Christ is with us, within us, beneath us, and around us—to enable us, in faith, to endure.

Our Lord Jesus Christ has promised that we shall prevail. *His plan of redemption shall succeed!* Both creature and creation will one Day, by the grace of God in Christ, come together to celebrate

The Gospel of Grace for Wounded Sojourners

His complete victory over every form of evil, in the establishment of the reign of God over all.

In this season of Advent we tell the world that evil can and will do its worst—but God will win the Day. Therefore: "... when these things begin to take place, stand up and lift up your heads, because your redemption is drawing near!" Amen.

Sixteen

Luke 2:51–52

He Obeyed His Parents

Then (Jesus) came down with (Mary and Joseph) and came to Nazareth and was obedient to them. His mother kept all these things in her heart. And Jesus increased in wisdom and stature, and in favor with God and people.

FOR THOSE PARENTS AND grandparents here this morning, who thought that, finally, they could nudge their child or grandchild and demand that he or she pay particular attention to this sermon—as it is about obedience, being well-behaved, listening to those adults with whom they are, in the words of our text, "obedient"—I must say—that's not where we'll be going. Perhaps we'll go in that direction with another passage, on another Sunday; but not this morning.

This morning there are other fish to fry!

After all, Luke does convey the "subjection" or obedience of Jesus to His parents, but only as an affirmation of Christ's profound humility and reverence for the purpose for which He'd come into this world. As Luke is one of only two gospels with, what has been called, a *birth narrative*, his story makes clear that both Mary and Joseph were well-aware of the divine origin of their first child's conception and birth.

In the movie, *The Nativity*, there's a captivating scene in which Mary and Joseph, as they make their way to the city of Bethlehem, take time for rest and refreshment. And while sharing the glow of a fire, they speak of this child in her womb, of what they know of His origins, of who He really is, and of what it'll mean for them as parents. At one point Joseph says: "I wonder what I could ever possibly teach Him." It's that sentiment that Luke is addressing when he states that Jesus "was obedient" to Mary and Joseph; which is also why it is said that Mary "kept all these things in her heart."

I cannot begin to comprehend the intensity of this experience in the lives of these two very common people—Mary and Joseph, called to be the earthly parents of the Messiah of Israel, the Son of Man, the Son of God. My admiration for them is amplified in knowing that—with an exemplary measure of faith in God and God's word—they willingly took-on the task of parenting His Son incarnate.

So—that's the first thing that must be said; knowing their first-born's origins, His unquestioned obedience to them was yet another *mystery* surrounding this entire event of His coming into the world. You see then why Luke tells us that Mary "kept all these things in her heart." What could be a more fitting and faithful response to having been called to take part in and to contribute to the great work of God for the salvation of the world? Mary treasured in her heart the fact that the Messiah—the long awaited Redeemer of Israel and the world—entered the world without fanfare and with such profound humility.

The Son of the living God, born in a common stable; his royal court composed of the most ordinary creatures; honored by those society deemed worthless was freely placing Himself in *subjection* to His earthly parents. If there's a lesson for all children in this part of Luke's narrative, I'd say it's this: If God's Son humbled Himself in free obedience, subjection to His parents, it's the height of pride or arrogance for any mere human child to disrespect parent(s)!

Luke 2:51–52

Throughout the history of the Church there have been numerous theologians who have referred to the first Advent of the Christ, the Incarnation of the Son of God, as God's *accommodating* humanity. John Calvin uses the same expression throughout his writings as a way of talking about the severity of grace; that is to say, the way in which the Son of God subjected Himself to the confinements of our human nature, taking-on Himself the consequences of sin as the way to salvation. God's grace—expressed as His love for us in Christ—comes at a cost to His heart that is unparalleled.

We Christians do not worship a God who is far removed and aloof to our common experiences of suffering and set-backs. Our Lord accommodated Himself to our human-condition, and in this way shared our sorrows. Yet, if the gospel story ended there, we would all be in serious trouble. We also know that salvation has come in Christ; that at the heart of human history there's been this event of Christ's incarnation, which has forever altered both the course and the end of human history. Were it not for the accommodation of Christ to our human condition under the power of sin, making salvation the reality of creature and creation—all would've been lost. That, my friends, is the bottom line.

Mary and Joseph were there even as the first chapter in this incredible narrative of God's accommodation to the human condition was written on the page of human history. They knew the origin of their child, and yet, took-on the task of parenting Him with all the devotion and care one expects of any "good enough" parent—even taking into consideration all the mystery of His person. I wonder if that isn't the reason Luke tells us that, "Jesus kept increasing in wisdom and stature (that is age), and in favor with God and with people."

It's, in some fashion, complementary of the parenting Mary and Joseph brought to the task of raising this exceptional Son. I suppose, in the familiar jargon of the typical Jewish household, Joseph and Mary ran a "kosher" home, and raised Jesus to come to the full measure of the person the gospels portray Him to have been. Why stress this factor? Only because I believe that, implicitly,

Luke is also making a theological claim for the need to maintain a family, a household, in good faith, with those devotional practices one associates with faithful worship of and service to God. So—tell me *that* theological claim lacks relevance for the time in which we live.

The implications are enormous, and in particular for those among us with young children who have somehow come to believe that the Christian church has little or nothing to offer in the formation of a child's character. You know as well as I that the time is long past when the Church held a higher place in the priorities of the family. Now, for many, the Church is merely one option among many bidding for time and commitment from the family. Much has changed, hasn't it? But what *hasn't* changed is the necessity for children to be raised in an environment that takes their souls as seriously as it takes their physical and intellectual achievements. Extra-curricular activities aside, recent surveys have demonstrated that children at all age levels spend far too much time with their technological-toys—and far too little time learning to relate to others.

In fact, just the other day I heard a report about the increase in fatal accidents with pedestrians during these late autumnal evenings—mostly children, who are distracted with an IPod or cell phone, or some other gadget—and walk directly into the path of an oncoming vehicle! It is tragic to see our children dying from such foolish use of technology, yet far more so to witness them losing the capacity to imagine, to dream, to create, which are all functions of the human soul—only because they hold in their hands a device that does it for them.

Yes, Jesus obeyed His parents; but it is just as important to recognize the influence of Mary and Joseph in raising this Child to become a person who gained such great favor with God and (others). It's a tribute to their parenting skills that Mary and Joseph raised such a Son.

I do not begrudge any parent the desire to see his or her son or daughter use those God-given talents and gifts given him or her; whether in some sport, or in pursuit of intellectual achievement.

Luke 2:51–52

It is also a tribute to parents who care in this way for the development of their child's character. I commend them.

What troubles me is the way in which the growth and development of the child's *soul* has now become secondary *at best*, if not purely-passé to many parents, remembering that in the biblical concept, the *soul* is the *self*—the very core of one's character—that which distinguishes one from another, as made *imago Dei*—in the image of God. So—would it be detrimental for contemporary parents to assume Mary and Joseph as role models of the very best parenting can be? I—*for one*—doubt it! Amen.

Seventeen

Luke 4:16–19
The Claim of Christ

The scroll of the prophet Isaiah was given to (Jesus), and unrolling the scroll, He found the place where it was written: "The Spirit of the Lord is upon Me, because He has anointed Me to preach good news to the poor. He has sent Me to proclaim freedom to the captives and recovery of sight to the blind, to set free the oppressed, to proclaim the year of the Lord's favor."

I'D LOVE TO LIVE in the kind of world Jesus describes in this morning's gospel lesson. Quoting, as He does, from the prophet Isaiah, Jesus describes a world in which all forms of physical malady are but a memory; and human life is lived in physical and emotional well-being. No longer are infants born with twisted limbs or tongues; wheelchairs and walkers are no longer a necessity; and all that we'd presently associated with human discord has been transformed and there's only total peace and harmony among people and nations.

Luke 4:16-19

Whenever I read this passage from Luke's gospel I feel melancholic, longing as I do for these words of Jesus to become the reality of the world in which we presently live. I suppose there're some who would judge my reaction to the words of Jesus far too emotional—more than a little naive! Nevertheless, that's the feeling I'm left with when I read the words from the first public sermon our Savior preached in His hometown of Nazareth.

Frankly, I think many of those in the synagogue that day probably felt the same; wondering—when? When would this world Jesus read about in the words of Isaiah become our truth, our reality, actual in our day-to-day living? When will this wonderful promise of God through the voice of His prophet, Isaiah, come to fruition and fulfill humanities deepest desire and pressing need?

When will the day come when we'll live in the world God promises: a world where no one is ever held captive to sickness or the heartache of loss; where tears always flow from a heart of joy and laughter; where children never need go to bed hungry, or sell their souls to be loved by someone—*anyone*; where all weapons of destruction are melted-down and used in the construction of play-grounds. When will we experience *that* world? Imagine—if you will—living in *that* world.

Regrettably, we don't, which is why these words of Jesus are so hard to hear. Well, actually, not so hard to *hear*, as to *believe*; to believe the world described will ever be the one you and I, or our grandchildren and great-grandchildren, for that matter, will ever experience. So often our world, the one to which we awaken each morning, is like a huge-festering-wound of senseless human suffering and set-backs. Interestingly, the same can be said of those who first heard these words on that Sabbath day in the synagogue in Nazareth.

It wasn't so much the words of the prophet Isaiah that caused them trouble; they'd heard the same passage read on countless occasions by their rabbi—yet always as a promise of what will one day be, a amazing dream awaiting realization, a vision of the world wished for, yet far from the day-to-day realities of life as they knew it. Had Jesus read and sat down—no problem.

The Gospel of Grace for Wounded Sojourners

What caused those gathered in that synagogue distress—mounting to anger—was the claim of Christ, when He asserted: "Today as you listen, this Scripture has been fulfilled." And, please, make no mistake about exactly what is being declared: It is not only the ministry of Jesus to which He is referring; it is in His person that the passage and promise from Isaiah is realized—now, in their presence. In Jesus, in His person and presence, the long and tortured history of human heartache has finally come to an end.

I'd imagine that seated in that same synagogue that morning were persons who knew, intimately, those same hardships Jesus was claiming had ended: a man, blind from birth; a woman embattled by demons; a child leaning on crutches; a family barely squeezing-by, with poverty crouching at their door; a man bruised from a Roman beating. And consider what might have been the cause of confusion and anger among the general population of that same synagogue on hearing Jesus make this outrageous claim: many burdened with taxes, draining them of what little savings they could muster; living each day beneath the jack-boot of Roman injustice and wondering when the arrest would come; others subject to diseases that could decimate an entire family almost overnight.

To this gathering of people Jesus made His incredible claim: "Today as you listen, this Scripture has been fulfilled." In brief: The anxious waiting and longing for God's promised relief and release had now ended—*now*—at that very moment, in the person of Jesus. Spiritual restoration, moral transformation, rescue from all kinds of demonic powers, deliverance from all forms of illness. All of that which was promised in and through the word of the prophet Isaiah—all present in the person of Jesus. That was the claim of Christ. Jesus claimed that in His person and by His power the heartache of each and every form of human suffering had now come to an end.

This claim of Christ would still be hard to swallow were it not for the witness of the Gospel itself to the wonders Jesus did perform: "the blind (received) their sight, the lame (walked), the lepers (were) cleansed, the deaf (were made to) hear, the dead (were)

Luke 4:16–19

raised (to life), and the poor (had) good news brought to them." The blind, lame, lepers, deaf, the dead? All? Not likely. Most? Not likely either. Many? Perhaps. Nevertheless, each wonder did testify to a miracle.

Each one served as a witness to the truth of the claim Christ made in that synagogue in Nazareth: As people now witnessed each wonder of healing, exorcism, and restoration of life, they knew they were witnessing the mystery of the hand of God healing human hurts through the word and touch of the Christ who'd made that outlandish claim. The question *isn't*, did Jesus open blind eyes, straighten twisted limbs, and call back the dead from captivity to the grave. The question is do we believe the Gospel witness to the wonders He performed? The question *isn't*, is that same Jesus with us in the power of the Holy Spirit. The question *is* will it be sufficient if He merely sustains us in and through our personal sufferings?

The question isn't, does God's faithfulness to each and all of His promises span the world like a rainbow. But rather, do we embrace the truth that we only need walk beneath that same rainbow—as a sign of our faith as trust—in order to receive God's blessings? For those who first heard Christ make that claim, as if he'd said: "The promise of God in the words of Isaiah have now come true in Me," it must've been difficult to get beyond their immediate skepticism.

And yet—as they came to witness one wonder after another, despair surely surrendered to delight, and doubt melted into devotion. And—now?

As someone has insightfully said, "Christ sees as no one else sees, with infinite and awful nearness; the agony of the dying, the prisoner's torment (and) the anguish of the wounded conscience. Injustice, terror, dread, and beastliness. Christ sees and hears and feels all this with the heart of a Savior." And where in our world is this the case? Where is that place in and through which Christ claims to "see and hear and feel" all of this "with the heart of a Savior?"

The Gospel of Grace for Wounded Sojourners

It's here—with you and with me as the Body of Christ. We are His eyes, His hands, His heart of compassion. If the world is to believe in the truth of what is claimed by Christ, it'll measure that truth by what it witnesses in the church, and what is done by the church in the face of human suffering and shame. Amen.

Eighteen

Luke 4:28–30
How do we hear Him

> When they heard (what Jesus had said), everyone in the synagogue was enraged. They got up, drove Him out of town, and brought Him to the edge of the hill that their town was built on, intending to hurl Him off the cliff. But he passed right through the crowd and went on His way.

WHILE I'VE EXPERIENCED SOME pretty strong reactions to sermons over the lifetime of my ministry, I can't recall a time when people just got-up from their pews and walked out of the sanctuary—much less taking me by the scruff of the neck and throwing me out-of-town! Then again—I have a number of sermons still under my belt, and, God only knows.

Nevertheless, the issue for us, as raised by this story of Jesus' first sermon, is far more critical. The setting for this story is vital, as the synagogue was located in the hometown of Jesus; in other words, these were people who were once His neighbors, perhaps even extended family members. And so, you can see how the severe reaction of those worshiping in the synagogue in which Jesus preached, took-on a more personal note than might otherwise have been the case. Harsh criticism and rejection from strangers is one thing; it's far more painful to the heart and soul when those who are overly-critical are friends and family.

I share this simply as a way for us to be clear about what Jesus meant when He said to them "no prophet is accepted in his hometown." In other words, His claim to be a prophet of God would have been sufficiently scandalous to raise the ire of the worshippers that day. But—of course—as we know the claim He made was far more radical.

The claim Jesus made that day was that He was the *fulfillment* of the words spoken by the prophet, Isaiah, one of Israel's most gifted, respected, and loved prophets. The writings of Isaiah were quoted and used far more than were any of the remaining prophetic writings; and it was in Isaiah that Israel came to anticipate the great Day of final deliverance, with the advent of God's Messiah. It was also a great honor to read the scripture for the day from the lectern of the synagogue—and so, Jesus knew that He would—at that moment—receive the undivided attention of His listeners.

Interestingly, when Luke tells us that the book of the prophet Isaiah was handed to Him—and significantly—He found the place where it was written, Luke is indicating that Jesus chose the passage to be read—a prerogative reserved for the rabbi alone. The point is to suggest that, from the beginning, Jesus was affirming His authority to read and interpret the Sabbath-scripture. That, in and of itself, would've caused some commotion in the congregation. These people were certain they knew exactly who Jesus was—despite any claim He might have made; they said, "Isn't this Joseph's son?" They were implying that Jesus was the "son of the local carpenter of Nazareth" and nothing more.

All of their preconceptions of both *who* Jesus was and *who* the Messiah would be, fulfilling the words of the prophet Isaiah, made it nearly impossible for them to hear what Jesus was proclaiming. It wasn't the first, nor would it be the last, time that the preconceived ideas of His listeners made it virtually impossible for

Luke 4:28-30

them to hear, believe, and embrace the proclamation of Jesus as Truth, whole Truth, nothing but Truth.

Before we look more closely at exactly how it is this story is relevant to our faith in Jesus as the Christ of God, let's hear— I mean really *hear*—the passage He read from the *Book of the Prophet Isaiah*. Jesus chose a passage from the sixty-first chapter of the prophet:

> The Spirit of the Lord is on Me,
> because He has anointed Me
> to preach good news to the poor.
> He has sent Me
> to proclaim freedom to the captives
> and recovery of sight to the blind,
> to set free the oppressed,
> to proclaim the year of the Lord's favor.

Yet, it wasn't so much the passage chosen, as it was the interpretation to follow that caused such great alarm among those gathered in the synagogue. Jesus followed the reading, saying: "Today, as you listen, this Scripture has been fulfilled." To suggest, as He does, that every word of Isaiah had now been—or better— *was* now *being*—fulfilled, was to make the singular claim to be the Messiah. Because in Jewish theology, the *person* and his or her *actions* were considered one-and-the-same; when Jesus made the assertion that the words of Isaiah had already been fulfilled—His hearers automatically knew He meant—*in Him*!

We shouldn't fault these synagogue worshippers for what, in fact, has been common, even in the Christian Church for most of its own history. They read the signs-of-the-times and saw violence, warfare, injustice, and the prevalence of diseases that were untreatable. Their world—very much like our own—exhibited few signs of the promised salvation they'd been taught to anticipate with the coming of God's Messiah. Small wonder they found it hard to hear and believe Jesus.

And, honestly now, isn't that the very same issue that causes many, both outside and within the Christian community, to question the veracity of the claims of the Gospel and the Church's message? When we look-out-at the world in which we live—some two millennia after the first Advent of Christ into this sphere—don't we sometimes wonder how His words, His message, His claims could possibly be justified in light of what we see, hear, and know of this world? One needn't jump to such conclusion based on a panoramic view of the world as it is; one need only focus on the personal pain, suffering, and crises that claim much of one's delight in life.

I'd be a wealthy man if I had a dollar for every occasion when a believer shared his or her doubts in light of personal anguish. Even the most personal and least obvious injustice can cause one to question the claim of Christ—even the claim made in His first sermon in the synagogue of His own hometown. It's no stretch to suggest that our voices could resonate with those in that worship service on the Sabbath in Nazareth. How are we to *hear*, so as to *believe* Christ? I mean, can we learn to hear Him in such a fashion that by hearing we lay-hold of His every word as *Truth*, and therefore, relevant to each and every aspect of life as we live it?

After all, the claim of Jesus, from this morning's gospel lesson, exceeds anything that a reasonable person would be expected to believe—then and now. So, what exactly is the internal mechanism by which we can truly *hear* Jesus' claim that, with His first Advent, everything really has taken-on a new and remarkable dynamic?

First and foremost, the means by which we can embrace and believe the claim of Christ is—*faith*. And by faith, the Christian Church has never meant some form of blind and unquestioned, or even unchallenged, acceptance. One cannot even claim to have faith, unless God has first planted such grace in the heart and soul. Faith is as much a gift of God as is forgiveness, or the promise of eternal life in His coming Kingdom. Faith isn't the internal capacity to affirm that which is otherwise absurd or inconceivable, and it isn't the irrational belief that "every day, in every way, things are getting better and better;" and it certainly isn't the ability to see "a silver lining behind every dark storm cloud."

Faith is the God-given capacity to entrust all into the hands of our Lord. And in order to do that, faith enables one—*first*, to embrace—without reserve—the message and ministry of Jesus, as authentically the fulfillment of each and every messianic-claim; and *second*, to live one's life in such a way that the world witnesses in the believer, a uniquely hopeful, and yes, courageous approach to the whole of life. As another has said, "The essence of faith is being satisfied with all God is for us in Jesus."

We *hear* Jesus when we live the faith God has given us, not as a refuge from reality, but rather—as Christ Himself disclosed—as the demand that we face reality, even with all of its difficulties, setbacks, and sufferings of the human heart. We *hear* Jesus when, like Him—even when life is shadowed by a cross—we abide in faith, hope, and a realistic love of life, as it is, in light of the eternal life God has promised and prepared. Amen.

Nineteen

Luke 9:30–31
Another Exodus

...(Jesus) took along Peter, John, and James, and went up on the mountain to pray... Suddenly, two men were talking with Him—Moses and Elijah. They appeared in glory and were speaking of (Christ's exodus), which He was about to accomplish in Jerusalem.

IF YOU WERE TO refer to other translations, you'd find that while some refer to the "departure" Jesus was about to accomplish in Jerusalem, others state that it was the "death" of Christ that he was about to accomplish in Jerusalem. The Greek, however, is far more subtle and equally striking; it's the term that's literally translated as "exodus." The associations with the history of the Jewish people are obvious and intentional.

The exodus from Egypt marked the beginning of Israel's worship of God. And not just any old god—but the God of Abraham, Isaac, and Jacob—the God of the covenant—the One who'd never forgotten His people, and, having heard their cries for mercy under

Luke 9:30–31

the vicious treatment of their taskmasters in Egypt, had finally come-down to deliver them from bondage.

While Moses, and his brother Aaron, were the instruments of deliverance, they could bring such freedom from captivity only because the Lord God was moved by the hardships of those closest to His heart, Israel.

The exodus has played a defining role in the entire history of the Jews, even to those who are contemporaries; it's the singular event used to characterize all that they believe and hold dear in devotions; making them extraordinary among all nations of the earth. In fact, it was this same characteristic that caused some in the Christian church to describe the Nazi Holocaust as a cruel wound inflicted on the apple of the Lord's eye! There can be no doubt that Israel were a people chosen by God to be and become the central focus of His attention and affection—and that hasn't changed, despite what some in the Church have mistakenly asserted. The Holocaust was, if the truth be told, fueled in part by a phrase attributed to the reformer, Martin Luther, who apparently referred to the Jews as "Christ-killers."

This extended introduction to the passage from the gospel, normally referred to as "the account of the transfiguration of Christ," is intended to create the strongest bond imaginable between the topic being discussed by Jesus, Moses, and the prophet Elijah—and the historical event of the exodus from Egypt. In other words, the connection is essential to the gospel story.

The exodus was as much a demonstration of God's devotion to the covenant made with father Abraham as it was the establishing event that created a nation from a mixed-bag-of-people, which is exactly what the name "Hebrew" means—a mixture of people from everywhere. It was the fulfillment of the Lord's promise to Abraham, to make of him a great and numerous nation, as much as it was a demonstration of God's faithful and steadfast love for *this* people in the act of their liberation from the chains and hard-labor of their former oppressors.

But such liberation, or in the more familiar language of our Christian faith—salvation—came not because there was some characteristic intrinsic to the Hebrews, but, again, and in the language of the reformers—such liberation came by grace and grace alone—not by merit. There is in the Old Testament as much "gospel" as there is "law" or commandment. Throughout her long and often painful history, Israel would point to the exodus event as an act that embodied "gospel"—and it was this "gospel" that then became the foundation for the entire "law" and all forms of obedience to the commandments of the Lord God. The people of Israel were summoned to obey the Lord based solely on His prior love for them, and on His faithfulness to the covenant made with Abraham, as evident in the *exodus* from slavery, injustice, and the hard-labor of their taskmasters.

Most of us have sufficient knowledge of the history of Israel to know how, with time, the form of obedience required of all people became an impossibility—too many laws of human fabrication, and too little leisure for engagement with these additional laws. So, as the people were unable to practice such a strict observance, the group known familiarly as the "Pharisees" took-up the role of obedience and strict observance of the entire law *for* the people—a kind of vicarious fulfillment of the *whole* law, done for the *whole* people, by the few.

However, this became an equal burden, as this group still required much of the people, and together with the priestly cult, known as the "Sadducees," made any and every observance of the faith a burden—a new form of bondage. Soon it was no longer the love of God that established the freedom of obedience, but obedience to the law that assured one of gaining the love of God. Jesus stated it dramatically with this admonition: "Woe also to you experts of the law! You load people with burdens that are hard to carry...." Jesus Christ came as the One to deliver, to liberate, to free all people from this tedious form of obedience, captured in that memorable phrase: "Come to Me, all you who are weary and burdened, and I will give you rest. All of you take up My yoke and learn from Me, because I am gentle and humble in heart, and you will find rest for yourselves. For My yoke is easy and My burden is light."

Luke 9:30–31

The gospel has proclaimed that, with the advent of Jesus Christ, the requirements of the law have been fulfilled in Him and by Him—once and for all who come to faith in Jesus as the Christ of God. That's, in part, the meaning of the common phrase—justification by grace through faith. It means that when we are in Christ, by faith we stand before God as if we'd never sinned—justified, fully. What a wonderful sense of genuine freedom to serve is ours, once we see that we've been liberated from any and every attempt to please God, or to "get-right-with" God on our own efforts and as a merit we can earn.

You see, in Jesus Christ there's been another—a *new* and more *inclusive exodus*; only this time we've been liberated from the bondage imposed by sin and its sting—that is to say, death. So we are told in the gospel of this celebrated event, in which Jesus is seen in all His glory, with Moses—the giver of the law and the first liberator of Israel, and Elijah—the one prophet whose return was believed—and by our Jewish friends, is still believed—to be forerunner to the coming of the Messiah. And they are sharing joy in discussing the *new* exodus about to come in Christ.

It's this *new* exodus, accomplished in Christ, which directly bears on our lives—even more on our dying and death. The new exodus made possible in and through Jesus Christ is the opening of the grave, the vacating of death's domain, known as "hades" in the scriptures, the conquest of every form of evil that would bring only death and destruction to God's creation.

For Peter, James, and John—the witnesses to the transfiguration of Jesus—the meaning of this event and the promise of a new exodus would've been veiled, as the resurrection of Christ was yet to come.

They came to realize the full measure of grace in this new exodus only after they became witnesses to the Risen Lord Christ. For all subsequent generations of believers—including each of us—we have the faithful testimony of those who saw the Risen Christ—wounds and all. Yet, like those first witnesses, for us this new exodus remains a promise—a promise in which we can invest every measure of faith—a promise witnessed in both the transfiguration and the events of Easter and beyond—and yet, a promise we wait to be fulfilled in the return of Christ and the establishment of God's reign in all the earth.

Regardless of the burdens we must shoulder in this life—and we all each of us shoulder life's hardships—we must hold firm in our faith in the Risen, Living, Reigning Lord Christ—and in the certainty that nothing, absolutely nothing can separate us from the love of God in Christ.

We live in the light of that *new* exodus—the Word of God in human flesh, who is our Liberator and our Lord; we live with the hope of the ultimate victory of Christ, a Day when our definitive deliverance will come—and God will be all in all. Amen.

Twenty

Luke 4:1–13
The Devil You Say!

The Jesus returned from the Jordan, full of the Holy Spirit, and was led by the Spirit in the wilderness for 40 days to be tempted by the Devil. He ate nothing during those days, and when they were over, He was hungry.

OF ALL THE PASSAGES in the four gospels that speak of the experiences of Christ during the sojourn of His earthly ministry, none can be said to be more relevant to the day-to-day living of the disciple than is the one passage before us this morning. Said differently, the temptations faced by Christ in the wilderness are a mirror image, and thereby symbolic, of those forms of temptation that are most common to the experience of Christian discipleship. Christ becomes the model for how all faithful souls are to cope with temptation.

While any one of us hasn't the weight of human redemption on our hearts and minds, as did Christ, temptation is still a very real and very *formidable* spiritual force with which we must contend each and every day of our walk of faith with Christ. That's why it's vital for us to understand how it is that Jesus—out there in the wilderness of Judea, alone in dealing with the forces of Satan—why it's vital we see how He dealt with temptation, assuring us that we too can be victorious over each and every moment of temptation, if we follow Christ's lead.

It's been said that each of the three forms of temptation Christ faced uniquely addressed His role as Messiah, as Savior; it was the Accusers way of drawing Christ into a struggle of the will—to see if Christ was sufficiently strong—in human flesh—to withstand Satan's assaults on His heart and soul. Yet, if the incarnation of the Son of God—if the Son of God taking-up our humanity in all its fullness, save for sin—if this truth touches on the deepest and most profound need of the human heart and soul—then we must also confess and believe that the temptations Christ faced, first in the wilderness, but also throughout His life on earth, were nothing less than a manifestation of the degree to which God the Son suffered as our Savior.

Perhaps it hadn't occurred to you prior to hearing it said—but *temptation*, in whatever form and under whatever circumstance it comes—is, for the disciple, as it was for the Lord, a source of *suffering* for the heart, soul, and spirit—and yes, sometimes even for the body—the physical nature—as well. And why is that so? Because temptation is the Satan's attempt to literally rip the believer away from the grace and love of God; to wound the soul. Temptation was as much a burden for Jesus as it is for each of us; even more so, as Christ was the Son of the living God, making each of many temptations He suffered all the more painful, as He could have avoided the mess of our human limitations and spiritual weaknesses, and remained in the glory of heaven.

God in Christ demonstrates the extreme vulnerability of the heart of our heavenly Father in exposing Himself to that form of suffering unique to the human soul—in other words, the Satan's attempts to tear-us-away from all that is good, holy, considerate, merciful, forgiving, and redemptive. Anyone who would confess to having been tempted will testify to how such spiritual assault on the heart and soul is no less painful than any one form of suffering

Luke 4:1-13

due to some physical impairment—*temptation* is the spiritual scalpel of Satan—slicing away.

Having stated in the most general of terms how it is that temptation itself is to be understood, we can turn to this morning's gospel lesson and unpack the importance of the three temptations Christ suffered while "being led by the Spirit in the wilderness" of Judea. In this instance, as in almost every single instance in the Scripture, *wilderness* is meant to be symbolic, the place of barrenness, gloom; an inhospitable environment—attended, we are told, by Satan's minions and other forms of evil. In other words, "wilderness" is biblical code language for a place where the soul and spirit are put-to-the-test.

The immediate relevance for us is this: Whenever we must travel through some experience that is—like a *wilderness*—threatening in so many ways—we are also and in the same setting extremely vulnerable—and Satan knows it. Because evil is a parasite, it must feed off the fears and weaknesses of human existence; the fact that we are prone to sin—and in particular when we are in a weakened spiritual condition—is the advantage Satan presumes to have over us. However, he always seems to forget that, for the Christian, the Spirit of Jesus Christ in the life of the believer issues as the empowerment to prevail—even over the strongest or most alluring temptation Satan chooses to employ.

It's in the fact that Christ endured in the three forms of temptation experienced in the *wilderness* that we have our greatest sense of spiritual security; as we will see in what follows, each of the three temptations is also representative of those we ourselves face as Satan attempts to rip-us from the heart of God and the hand of Christ. We'll consider each in order, and then see their relevance for us.

The passage tells us that at the end of the forty days in the wilderness Christ was famished; and famished is the term intended to describe a physical condition far more severe than the hunger pangs of having missed lunch. The depth and degree of the hunger Christ felt could only be captured by use of the term *hungry,* or as it's rendered more accurately in another translation—*famished.* So it is that the *first* temptation Satan uses is to address the vulnerability of extreme physical need: "If You are the Son of God, tell this stone to become bread!"

And to avoid any misunderstanding, Satan does not doubt Jesus is the Son of God—because in each of the three temptations, the Satan's charge could more accurately be translated:

"*Because* you *are* the Son of God" do this, that, or the other thing. That puts a different spin on the words of Satan—wouldn't you say? Christ had chosen to place Himself in this posture of vulnerability through the extreme fasting demanded of any prophet in preparing himself to serve God's will—but also and equally important—Christ fasted until He was famished so that He could empathize with the greatest needs a human can face in life and in this world. It's far more than ironic that the Satan suggests turning a stone into bread, as Jesus will perform many miracles of a similar kind in His ministry—but only and always as a manifestation of God's mercy and provision.

It's at the point of our greatest vulnerability, our most pressing need, our deepest discouragement we need to recall the claim of Christ in response to this temptation: "Man must not live on bread alone." Notice, He did not say we'll never need "bread," which would be absurd. But even our greatest need cannot be met materially alone. Even in the depths of our most desperate circumstance—whether it be a threat to our physical well-being, our emotional welfare, or our sense of security—in the depths of such desperation, when the Satan comes to tempt us to seek solace in something—anything merely material, we must recall Christ's own extreme hunger and His resilient words. There's a far greater need for the human heart, soul, mind, and spirit—and that is, of course, the necessity to entrust one's self, and in particular under the most dire of circumstances, into the loving, gracious, and benevolent will of our heavenly Father, as did Christ.

The *second* of Satan's temptations—you'll no doubt recall—was the offer of the riches of all the kingdoms of the world, if Christ would fall down and do homage to Satan. Here the relevance is less obvious but not less critical. After all, consider the implied options

Luke 4:1–13

Satan has presented our Lord; He can bask in all the glory, riches, and power of worldly rule—but only at the price of giving His very soul to the Satan. Now the relevance becomes strikingly clear:

It's the same alternative Satan places before believers—even in our contemporary world. No, we may not be offered all the kingdoms of the world—but Satan still tempts us with whatever we think will assure our success in life, or secure for us recognition, or advance our need to control, or feed us with an inflated sense of self-importance. Yet, we weren't created to rule the world, or to receive the esteem and adulation of devotees, or to spend a lifetime seeking power, wealth, or social standing. We were created for communion with God, to worship God and *God alone*, and to serve His cause through our devotion to His Christ.

Finally, when all else failed, the Satan tempted Christ to a game of "Russian roulette" with the gracious love and protection—that is to say—the providential goodness God intends for each and all of His children. The irony in this scene is that the Satan was right; it was in fact true that the angels would have upheld Christ so that the fall taken wouldn't have been fatal. But again—at what cost?

This isn't all that far removed from the experience most, if not all, Christians have had or will have—present company included. That's the tendency, from time-to-time to attempt to strike a bargain with God. I'm certain you already know what I'm referring to; putting the love and grace of God to "the test" by trying to squeeze-out an agreement—something like, "Do this for me, God. . .and I promise I'll never, or, I'll always. . .!" A ludicrous thing to suggest—right?

Christ simply stated another fact—it's foolish to place God in the position of being responsible for the consequences of the choices we've made; whether sound or silly choices is irrelevant to the claim of Christ: God is not to be bargained with under any circumstance; it belittles God's sovereignty and gracious good will as it also and at the same time undercuts confidence in the veracity of God's promises, and the steadfast love God has for His own.

The Gospel of Grace for Wounded Sojourners

What we learn from the temptations faced by our Lord is that He was willing, with a profound love, to experience and internalize the suffering of temptation as a tool of Satan to tear and shred the relationship we have with God. But we also learn that Christ was victorious over each temptation, proving His power that much superior to Satan's claims. And that—most assuredly—is "Good News!" Amen.

Twenty-One

John 2:1–12
Why Wine?

Jesus performed this first sign in Cana of Galilee. He displayed His glory, and His disciples believed in Him.

RECENTLY A COLLEAGUE, IN commenting on the sermon title for this evening, said, "That's a strange question—'why wine?' After all," he went on to say, "it was a wedding reception—and we all know how the alcohol flows at those galas!" And, of course, he's correct, isn't he. If there's a commonality, across all social and cultural barriers, when it comes to wedding festivities, that which is *most* common is the abundance of alcohol as a stimulant to celebration. Of course, at the time of Jesus, it was wine which was the universal beverage of choice for even everyday meals.

It only stands to reason then that wine was prevalent at every wedding reception; but even at the most elementary level of use, wine also had symbolic importance. As the grape of wine grew on a vine, it suggested that wine was the beverage of unity and being a community; as wine was also a stimulant, it implied spiritual ecstasy; and as wine was—more often than not—red in color and rich in flavor, it was thought to symbolize the richness and vibrancy of life.

Other than its use in social settings, I believe most of this symbolic meaning has been lost on us.

What's, perhaps, *most* fascinating about this text from John's gospel—a story with which we, most of us, are familiar—is the manner in which "wine" is used to symbolize a much higher, a more transcendent, a superior reality; one that is both present in the ministry of Jesus, and yet, awaiting *ful*fillment in the future. Rather than begin with the "wine"—it's significant that this particular wine is being imbibed at a wedding; in other words, the setting for this "first sign" performed by Christ, is almost as important as the wine itself.

Weddings and the associated joyous festivities had been used throughout the history of Israel as an illustration of everlasting joy, to be experienced in God's coming kingdom, where a "new family of faith" will be formed and celebrated as well. Just as any wedding—then or now—represents a new beginning and the promise of love's enlargement, so it also came to represent the originality of communion in God's coming kingdom and the everlasting nature of the love God would make available to all who were invited to this wedding and its related festivities. As a wedding holds *promise* of children—so the kingdom, as God's wedding, would disclose His children.

It's possible that, even though invited, Jesus had attended this particular wedding, at Cana-in-Galilee, with the full intent of using the occasion to disclose a reality that those in attendance would never have thought possible—His disciples included. And I'm not simply referring to the so-called miracle or sign of changing water-into-wine. That event—as striking and incredible as it was—would have meant nothing to anyone even ten years after the occurrence, had it not held within it a truth, far beyond the boundaries of its own time and place.

And that is the significance of the sermon title and the question posed: "Why wine?"

John 2:1-12

Let's begin then with what is, perhaps, the symbolic use of "wine" that is most commonly associated with Christians and their ritual practice of the Eucharist, or Holy Communion. There're several reasons why Christians have always used "wine" or the "fruit of the vine" as one of two elements in this sacrament; all of them having to do with Christ, and all of them mandated by Scripture. The most obvious reason is because it was the custom of the Jews to use wine at the Passover festival—and chances are, when Jesus instituted the service of Holy Communion, wine was used at table.

Even more to the point is the way in which Christ re-defined the "wine" as his "blood" or as "the blood of the new covenant" shed for the forgiveness of sins. So, both the "bread" and the "wine" became associated with the *person* of Christ; so much is that the case, that when broken and poured-out in worship, they are said to make Christ's presence with His people a reality. It isn't simply that communicants "remember" Christ—but He is *present* in a profound way. In this manner "wine" became symbolic of Christ's blood—His sacrifice of shed blood on the cross—and the very substance of His life. Together with the broken bread, the wine became an emblem of Christ's body. The apostle Paul went so far as to associate the celebration of communion, and the elements, with the Church as the "body of Christ." To the Church in Corinth Paul wrote:

"The cup of blessing that we give thanks for, is it not a sharing in the blood of Christ? The bread that we break, is it not a sharing in the body of Christ? Because there is one bread, we who are many are one body, for all of us share that one bread" (1 Cor. 10:16-17).

Wine continued to play an essential symbolic role in the entire worship life of the Church, representing not only the "life-blood" of Christ—if you will—but also came to be associated with the joy and festivity of faith in the salvation the shed blood of Christ had brought for all people. Even so, the prevailing significance of "wine" continued to be associated with the coming kingdom of God, which the New Testament writers proclaimed to have been made visible in the life, ministry, death, and resurrection of Christ. Christ's rule as Lord would last until the Day when the kingdom of God would be established in all the earth. It was with "glad and generous hearts" that the early Christians looked to the return of Christ and the establishment of God's kingdom in all its glory.

Returning then to our text from John's gospel; when he tells us that in this deed of turning water into wine Jesus "displayed His glory," he's asserting that this one act of Christ was a disclosure—in the present—of the reality of the kingdom of God in the future, as a feast of joy and new beginnings. The extreme amount of wine offered by Jesus is yet another representation of the abundance that will be made available to all in the coming kingdom of God; an abundance, that is, of all that we'd associate with a rich, rewarding, and full life—things like love, care, companionship, joy, laughter, and the presence of Christ in all His fullness as well.

"Why wine (?)": Because Christ knew only too well that wine was the one substance that everyone at that wedding would have associated with life, God's kingdom, and unparalleled joy. The family, His followers, the guests at that wedding—all would've recalled the words of the prophet Isaiah: "The LORD of Hosts will prepare a feast for all the people on this mountain—a feast of aged wine, choice meat, finely aged wine" (Isa. 25:6). And here's the promise the people of God had taken to heart—awaiting the Day of its fulfillment—perhaps we're still waiting; Isaiah proclaimed further: "On this mountain He will destroy the burial shroud, the shroud over all the peoples, the sheet covering all nations; He will destroy death forever. The LORD GOD will wipe away the tears from every face and remove His people's disgrace from the whole earth, for the LORD has spoken" (Isa. 25:7-8).

By the way—that closing phrase—"The LORD has spoken"—was intended to supplant the phrase then used by rulers the world over; whenever they issued a decree, it would be followed by the phrase: "So let it be written; so let it be done!"

Isaiah is saying that because the Lord has spoken it will—one Day—be done. And Jesus reclines at a wedding feast in the village of Cana-in-Galilee, and in creating the finest wine ever tasted by the steward of the wedding, and in such abundance that it amounts to hundreds of gallons, He has disclosed how it is that He is at the

John 2:1–12

very *center* of that same promise of God. Christ is the kingdom in the *flesh*—and His gift of so much wine is His way of asserting that "sadness and sorrow may linger for the night (of our sojourn on this earth), but absolute joy will come in the morning" of God's coming kingdom.

May I be permitted to voice it in this way: I believe that the Christian is a supreme slave to *hope*—*hope* as the richest *wine* in his or her life—superior *wine* as the enthusiastic *joy* by which he or she lives—new *wine* as the intoxicating worship of and devotion to the one Lord Christ—fresh *wine* as living witness to the promise of God's coming kingdom which will not fail. Amen.

Conclusion

IT SEEMS MORE THAN appropriate that the concluding sermon in this series should be one that was preached to the congregation gathered for the glorious celebration of the holy Eucharist, with its sacramental realities and its supremely important symbolism, not to mention the characteristic of celebrating a present manifestation of the coming kingdom of God in this *feast* of bread broken and cup poured-out. It's also fitting to end the series on this note as an affirmation of the *protestant principle* of the unity of Word and Sacrament, fundamental to the proclamation of Christ and the Gospel, while affirming the nature of the Church catholic as evident in the unity of the Body. Preaching takes on a unique form whenever its presentation comes within a worship service where the Eucharist is celebrated; both sermon and sacrament contribute to the manifestation of the *real presence* of the One whose identity cannot be divorced from either the message of the Gospel or the sacramental-representation of Him who is Lord of the Church.

When used for meditation and reflection, sermons demonstrate the superior quality of this particular form of writing in which Scripture and contemporary context are brought together to engage in a symbolic conversation, as the pastor-to-preach both listens, attentively, and contributes from the treasure-store of his or her own pastoral experience(s). There's really no other form of communication quite like preaching, and when it's done with devoted interest given to both process of preparation and eventual presentation, the result can be a moment of redemptive healing

Conclusion

for those who have *ears to hear*. In all of the duties to which one is committed, by virtue of his or her vows of ordination to the pastoral office, there's none as daunting or as delightful as that of taking-up the mantle of the preacher; it's a wonderful disclosure of a pastor's heart and soul.

A related area of joy for the pastor as preacher is located in the use of this unique form of language; a language that resonates with the realities of day-to-day existence, and yet, bears within it—like a clay pot—a transcendent treasure, which is never at the disposal or the control of the one sermonizing. This form of language is shaped by the presence of the Holy Spirit, as the wax of the preacher's human word is molded to conform to the image of Christ's own preaching, and is therefore heard as the healing Word of the One who is Lord of even this worshipful event of proclamation. No other language—not even that of the liturgy in general—can claim to bear the full weight of this immense truth; preaching is the precise moment of a merciful and medicinal Word for the soul seated in the pew; and is so as a reflection of what has already transpired for the pastor in his or her study while devoted to preparation.

Finally, the event of preaching—the content of the sermon itself—is a disclosure of the deepest theological commitment(s) of the one preaching. There is a general knowledge afoot in the Church catholic that a substantive theology has fallen silent; there's a sense in which Christians in general and across confessional lines are becoming incapable of expressing their faith in clear and concise theological categories. One can rightly assume that when and where this is the reality of the local congregation, preaching becomes little more than a review of the latest news, peppered with some catchy clichés, and topped-off with a personal point-of-view from the perspective of the one in the pulpit—not always the pastor. Deep and deliberate theological reflection is essential to both the integrity of preaching and the substantive character of the Christian disciple; there's clearly no substitute for the hard work of theological study and the development and maturation of one's own theological character as a pastor in office. To that extent reading the sermons of another can become a vehicle for developing the skills necessary for offering a theological critique—and therefore a *constructive* assessment—of the form and content of the preaching event. Any preacher worthy of the title would welcome such a *theological assessment* of his or her efforts.

Since I have chosen not to have an *Acknowledgment* page, I express my gratitude to Carolyn Crouthamel for her willingness to spend more time on the selection of sermons and proofing of this manuscript than could rightly be expected of anyone, much less someone who already offers much to her church, family, community, and friends. I also want to express appreciation to Mrs. Helen Godshall (a member of Heidelberg), whose thoughtful, insightful, and generous commentary on hundreds of my sermons has served to strengthen my commitment to take ever more seriously the need for more careful preparation of sermons and reflective regard for greater clarity of expression—not to mention her wonderful theological insights. I also could name numerous others who have shared comments, constructive criticism, and even an occasional disappointment, but always with the tone of Christian affection and genuine graciousness.

We will, together as pastors-who-preach, continue to develop as those Christ has called to this office and its respective ministries; and we will rejoice in the knowledge that one sermon does not a pastoral heart make or disclose—there's always time for repentance and refreshment of this superior art of preaching—as we seek to proclaim the *whole counsel of God*.

www.ingramcontent.com/pod-product-compliance
Lightning Source LLC
Chambersburg PA
CBHW050836160426
43192CB00010B/2045